Give Love A-Way

How to Fellowship with the Holy Spirit

Karen Loring

Give Love A-Way
How to Fellowship with the Holy Spirit

First Edition – 2021
Copyright © 2021 Karen Loring
All rights reserved.

No part of this manuscript may be used or reproduced in any manner whatsoever without written permission from the Author, except in the case of brief quotations embodied in critical articles and reviews; excluding all quotes followed by the phrase 'Word of Wisdom.'

For permissions or more information please email: contact@givelovea-way.org

Unless otherwise stated, Scriptures taken from the Holy Bible, New International Version®, NIV®. Copyright © 1973, 1978, 1984, 2011 by Biblica, Inc.™ Used by permission of Zondervan. All rights reserved worldwide. www.zondervan.com The "NIV" and "New International Version" are trademarks registered in the United States Patent and Trademark Office by Biblica, Inc.™

British Library Cataloguing in Publication Data

A catalogue record for this book is available from the British Library.

ISBN: (Paperback) 978-1-80049-098-7

Edited by Heritage Editing Services
Email: editor@heritageediting.co.uk

Stories and practical advice on YouTube Channel: Give Love A-Way2

Positive stories and constructive comments are welcome on Facebook: @GiveLoveAWay2

Thanks

'One of them, when he saw he was healed, came back, praising God in a loud voice. He threw himself at Jesus' feet and thanked him...' Luke 11:15-16

Jesus, thank you for coming to the earth, for Your obedience to the Father, and for choosing to die for us. Thank you for rescuing us from brokenness and selfishness. Thank you for giving me life.

Father, thanks for loving the world so much that You gave your Son to die for us. Thank you for unfailing love, and for sharing Yourself with us through Jesus. Thank you for showing me life.

Holy Spirit, thank you for sharing the riches of God with us, for choosing to live in us, love us, transforming us more into the likeness of Jesus. You are beautiful, thank you. Thank you for being life in me.

Mum and Dad – For ongoing love, friendship – love and thanks

In alphabetical order:

Barbara Dean – *For sharpening and laughter*
Chris and Penny Smith – *For love and lasting friendship*
Claire Tracey – *For courage, wise counsel, and for overcoming*
Family – *For being there when we need each other*
Jenny and Raymond Buick – *For the gift of friendship, learning, and quality time*
Kingsland Church – *For being beautiful, marvellous and encouraging*
Lucy Smith – *Forever family; loved, valued and respected*
Neil Loxley – *For safe and inspiring leadership*
Paul Bonham – *For unfailing loyalty, love, and inspiration*
Toyin Onabowu – *For generosity, and wise editorial insight*

FOREWORDS

Lori Arnott Lawlor

Leader, Harvest Ministries UK
Founder, Spirit Cafe International

www.harvestministries.co.uk

I would never have considered myself an evangelist. Until recently, I always preferred ministry in the church - not ministry to strangers! I found Christian-sounding ways to justify this, but, really, it was fear.

I remember the day the Holy Spirit changed everything. After many years of building and leading church, putting much of what I had learned regarding prophetic words for people into practice, and doing all the things Christians who loved Jesus did, I remember the day the Holy Spirit changed everything.

As a church, we once held an outreach in the park near us. At the beginning of my turn on the 'prophecy in the park' teams, the first woman walked towards us. Immediately the Holy Spirit said to me,

"I want you to lead this person to Jesus."

"But, Holy Spirit, that's not what we're doing today." I replied.

"I know,' He said. "But that's what I'm doing today."

"Okay," I said. "Well, I want to do what You're doing."

In that one-hour slot, eight people gave their lives to Jesus; beginning new lives with Him! I only asked them, in simple language, to respond to the pictures and words given them, and they were all wanting to pray; wanting Him. I have to tell you I was so thrilled, but also shocked!

Obviously, it was a very exciting afternoon - and a huge wake-up call for me. Somewhere along the way, I had forgotten a few things. I forgot that God was searching for and loving His kids that didn't know Him yet, and that He was already working in their lives.

The second thing I forgot is that people are actually looking for Him. They're not looking for rules, regulations, or their experiences of judgmental Christians. They are searching for Him; for genuine, powerful encounters with His love and kindness.

Thirdly, I had forgotten that those who hadn't met Him yet would also appreciate such GREAT NEWS! That was a defining moment; a mindset changing moment. More and more, I and my team have observed the 'hungry ones' looking for Him in so many wrong places. They aren't queueing at our church doors, but nonetheless, they are around. If they aren't coming to us, we need to go to them.

I met Karen a number of years ago and recognised in her someone genuine and truly hungry for more of Jesus. I could tell she wanted to look and act more like Him. I found *Give Love A-Way* very refreshing. Karen has woven into its pages an authentic look at her personal journey and that of various teams she has led, into loving others. She recounts some great stories of victory and *'hurray!',* but also, things she would have liked a 're-do' on. She takes evangelism from being a scary, 'not for me' thing, to helping you see it as a very do-able, exciting and necessary part of our life in Jesus. I found myself cheering her on, and being encouraged to take every opportunity where the Holy Spirit leads me into loving others on His behalf.

What about you? Are you tired of simply occupying your Christian chair? Do you want to be challenged into action? Are you ready for some of your own 'evangelism mindsets' to be changed? Are you ready to take your training and gifting to those truly hungry ones? Are you ready to feel the Father's heart for those He is longing for, and as the Bible describes, 'be moved with compassion' towards those He longs for?

Don't let fear, personality, the past, or whatever, disqualify you from this wonderful partnership with God. May I encourage you, as Karen is about to do, to put your hand in the hand of the Holy Spirit, and love the one in front of you. As we step out, we discover how faithful He is, in a way that we can't otherwise learn.

David and Christine West

Bethel Sozo UK

www.bethelsozouk.org.uk

Jesus made flesh is His chosen way of communicating the gospel. He has not changed His mind. He continues to communicate the gospel through flesh and blood – this time it looks like you.

For this reason, as important as words will always be, the gospel must be more than words. Since the Gospel is the good news of Jesus and about Jesus, the Gospel we share must be the same Gospel that Jesus brought. As it was with Jesus, people can still experience the goodness of God—an important step in their journey to full revelation and salvation. The disciples journeyed with Jesus for some considerable time, saw many miracles and were even a part of those miracles, before they believed.

Karen has understood that salvation is a journey. No matter how dramatic it may appear, there is always a back story. Those who study such things tell us that people typically have seven "God moments" in their journey. A conversation, a church visit, an answer to prayer—everybody has prayed at some point in their life—whenever we share the gospel, we may reap sometimes, but much of the time, we sow.

I heard an evangelist tell a story about a coffee encounter. Leading a mission trip with a team, he was enjoying a well-deserved coffee and conversation with a friend. You have probably had one of those moments where, no matter what you are trying to do or supposed to be doing, God grabs your attention with something else. God kept directing his attention to a lady on a table opposite, and eventually he, wisely taking a friend with him, went over and started a conversation.

"Good afternoon, my name is J. I am a Christian and I believe that God wants to bless you. Is there anything I can pray about for you?"

She looked a little surprised but not worried and replied, "normally I would say no, but you are the third person today to offer to pray for me, so I guess I should say "yes". Pray they did and she experienced Heaven's intervention into her situation.

Who knows that the first two people who offered to pray for her that day got told 'NO' and, perhaps, went away feeling they had failed? They would soon learn the whole story when the team met together at the end of the day. Far from failing, they were an important part of her journey to experiencing God's goodness.

We need to resist the lie that we always have to be step seven in someone's journey. Be obedient to Heaven's prompting and be somebody's step one or step six. Occasionally, you will be their final step into the Kingdom of God. Enjoy those moments and keep an eternal perspective on all the conversations that seemed like failure. You won't know the whole picture until eternity, when you will enjoy Heaven's "well done", some of which will surprise you.

Karen has similar stories—all of which display Heaven—that come wrapped in her own vulnerable humanity. My favourite story, where she was happy to be a step in someone's—probably long—journey, is Matt in Chapter five.

While this book is not short on very practical suggestions, it is no simple "How to..." handbook, as much I find those useful. Karen writes "don't do evangelism, be evangelism". For this reason, she explores profound issues that shape who we are and, therefore, the gospel we represent. Reading this book will help you on your journey to be "naturally supernaturally evangelistic".

I especially appreciated the chapters on the Holy Spirit, mostly because all the evangelism Jesus did was in response to the Holy Spirit. He is as much God as the Father and Jesus, and He wants a relationship—a friendship—with us. I love the power, anointing, gifts, and fruit of the Spirit – all of that good stuff—but Paul's prayer was for the "Grace of the Lord Jesus, the love of God and the fellowship of the Holy Spirit". There is something to be learned, understood, experienced and enjoyed – fellowship for its own sake, devoid of agenda or task.

There is no shortage of pastors, teachers and even prophets and apostles in our churches. Not so with evangelists. They seem like a separate species from the rest of us. Karen dismantles such unhelpful stereotypes that keep this gift 'out of reach' of normal people.

Understanding that God loves your unsaved friend on their worst day, as much as He loves you on your best day, is a key to unlocking our motivation. "God so loved..." is at the heart of the Gospel, and it must be at the heart of the gospel we share.

Tony Maxwell, DVM, MDiv

Administrative Director
Iris Global Harvest School of Mission

www.irisglobal.org

Many are the books written concerning how to live the Christian life. While many reflect the viewpoint of Martha, – 'the doing' aspect, Karen approaches the topic from the vantage point of Mary, who viewed the 'being' aspect as more important.

Karen puts forth a startlingly simple and practical plan to walk in the presence and power of the Holy Spirit, both in one's personal journey with Jesus (loving God) and in reaching out to a lost and dying world needing the hope of the Gospel (loving people).

Raymond Buick, FRCS

A Friend

Karen is not just in love, she is betrothed; has promised to love, honour and obey. She is 'sold out', 'head over heels' and 'hopelessly in love' (hopeless from the enemy's standpoint) with Jesus.

The only way you know you are absolutely full is when you overflow.

When Jesus was on earth, he mentored the disciples. He was developing a church leadership outside the synagogue that could carry the message and lifestyle of the Kingdom in themselves. Jesus taught his disciples to be good examples of the Kingdom Lifestyle.

Someone once said that knowledge without experience is not Truth. Jesus has given us the Holy Spirit to lead us into all Truth.

In this book, Karen reveals her heart; being love to others. She tells her story. She shares her experience. She is walking the walk. She is an evangelist. She lives as a zealous advocate of her faith.

If you want more than advice or instruction, if you want to be inspired, and encouraged – read this book.

Put it on your good reading list.

You'll love it.

Contents

FOREWORDS

    Lori Arnott Lawlor - **Harvest Ministries UK**

    David and Christine West - **Bethel Sozo UK**

    Tony Maxwell - **Iris Global Harvest School of Mission**

    Raymond Buick - **A friend**

CHAPTER 1 – THE IMPORTANCE OF HIS PRESENCE 1
  New Beginnings 1
CHAPTER 2 – INTIMACY WITH THE HOLY SPIRIT 19
  Who is He Really? 19
CHAPTER 3 – IRIS HARVEST MISSION SCHOOL 21 27
  Dancing with the Holy Spirit 27
CHAPTER 4 – THREE WAYS OF BEING 41
  Knowing Who You Really Are 41
    When did we lose our power? 46
    We must get to know the Holy Spirit 47
    How Deep Is Your Fellowship with The Holy Spirit? 54
CHAPTER 5 – THE TESTIMONY OF JESUS 57
  An Emerging Story 57
    Surrender Isn't Weakness 64
CHAPTER 6 – THE TWO TREE KINGDOM 67
  Grow Fruit from the Tree of Life 67
    Choose to Look Through the Lens of Love 72
CHAPTER 7 – RECOGNISING THE OPPORTUNITY 75
  Whose is Your Life? 75
    What is our purpose on this planet? 82
    Who is leading us? 84
CHAPTER 8 - DESENSITISATION AND DISCONNECT 85
  How to Heal 85

    Existing or living? 88
    How far does His presence in you extend? 95
CHAPTER 9 – JESUS' VIEWS ON THE HOLY SPIRIT **99**
  Discovering the Fullness of God 99
    The Role of The Spirit is Defined by His Names 107
    Techniques for Abiding 112
CHAPTER 10 – KNOW YOUR IDENTITY **115**
  Post Resurrection Lifestyle 115
    Who You Really Are Is Who Jesus Really Is 115
    SEVEN STEPS FOR FINDING YOUR TRUE IDENTITY 118
    1. *Jesus Devoured the Word* 119
    2. *Jesus Cultivated Intimacy with His Father* 120
    3. *Jesus Became His Identity* 121
    4. *Jesus Walked in His Purpose* 122
    5. *Jesus Worked His Inheritance* 123
    6. *Jesus Trusted the Plan* 123
    7. *Jesus Partnered with Heaven* 124
CHAPTER 11 – CHOOSING PROPHETIC VISION **125**
  Look Through the Kingdom Lens of Love 125
CHAPTER 12 – REACHING OUT THROUGH THE HOLY SPIRIT **139**
  New Possibilities for Us All 139
CHAPTER 13 – STICKING PLASTERS ON LEPERS **147**
  Chocolates, Dreams, Tattoos and Streets 147
CHAPTER 14 – HOW TO WALK IN THE SPIRIT **189**
  He is *your* Holy Spirit 189
    1. *Seek First His Kingdom and His Righteousness* 189
    2. *Know Your Place on This Planet* 191
    3. *Practice Surrender* 193
    4. *Live from Your True Identity* 195
    5. *Live Holy* 198
    6. *Fellowship with The Holy Spirit* 199
    7. *Be Filled* 200
APPENDICES **203**

CHAPTER 1 – THE IMPORTANCE OF HIS PRESENCE

New Beginnings

An Introduction

There we all were, one crisp and sunny day in October, five students packed tightly into an old, yellow, under-powered 2CV Citroen. We were on our way to Bradford to experience a Bradford City Football Club match for the first time. Our decision to go to the game had been spontaneous. I was wedged, with two others, into the back seat on the driver's side. A buzz of excitement filled the air as we laughed and joked, anticipating the game, the atmosphere, the crowd.

Then it happened. It's so clear in my mind, even now. Stuck in traffic in a small rural Yorkshire town centre that was heaving with people and shoppers, I saw him from the car window. A tall man, walking through the crowds, but somehow, the focus of everyone's attention. A friendly, relaxed smile on his face, a wave of laughter moved with him as he talked with the people he went past.

I was curious. Was he famous? I watched more intently as the car edged forward in the traffic.

The impact on those around him was like a ripple. They turned to look at him and made laughing comments in his direction. I was puzzled and stared hard. He exuded a fascinating charisma, and there seemed to be a joy in the air that the changed atmosphere as he moved.

As we drove on, the man eventually passed out of sight, having touched my world in a profound way in that old yellow car. It was a moment caught in time.

This man is so fitting to this introduction. But who was he? What did he have? How did he command such presence? It's still puzzling all these years later; that man I never met, but whom I experienced so tangibly from such a distance. What did he have that attracted and engaged others so easily?

He appeared to have an intangible 'something else' that impacted people in his path, even me, from a distance. It was real and memorable.

As I anticipated writing this book, what the man in Yorkshire had suddenly hit me: *presence.* He looked, laughed and smiled like love, and this created a wave that touched the crowd around him. Possibly just like Jesus? Then, it occurred to me that we also have a gift: God's 'Presence' with and in us. The Holy Spirit, or Spirit of Jesus (as Paul occasionally calls Him in the New Testament) within us and on us, is the difference we carry, whether in a crowd or one to one.

Every Christian has this unique gift, in the form of the Presence of God through the Holy Spirit. You are a sign and a wonder. Atmospheres shift and people are drawn to the light of Jesus in you. When you have the Presence of Jesus, everyone and every situation around you will be influenced for the good.

This book emerged from a number of reasons. The following questions had begun to disturb me.

- Where has the power gone that should be normal in our lives as Christians?
- How do we achieve intimacy with the Holy Spirit?
- Can we have a relationship with the Holy Spirit?
- What difference will a relationship with the Holy Spirit make in our lives?
- How will His Presence in us enable us to reach out to others on a daily basis?

Let's travel on a learning journey together into Love. Let's discover our true identity as carriers of His Presence through relationship with the Holy Spirit and His equipping.

It's going to be a great journey during which you can expect to be changed as you discover more.

A Journey of Becoming

> *"I will not leave you as orphans; I will come to you. Yet a little while and the world will see me no more, but you will see me. Because I live, you also will live. In that day you will know that I am in my Father, and you in me, and I in you." John 14:18-20*

My grandmother was so important during my childhood and adulthood. She not only loved Jesus with all her heart, her eyes shone with a love that made a huge impression on me. It influenced my growing up and finding Jesus. Hers was an unconditional love that promoted courage and confidence, and offered acceptance and safety. Nan was my childhood hero right until she left her earthly body to be with Jesus.

One evening, when I was about 4 or 5, Nan encouraged me to say my prayers as she put me to bed. I had no idea how or what to pray. I remember her clasping my tiny fingers together in her hands, inviting me to close my eyes and suggesting I pray through a list of family names: 'God bless Mum, God bless Dad, God bless my brother Richard...' etc. The prayers happened most nights until many years later when I encountered and began a relationship with Jesus.

'The best thing we can gift to another human being is the knowledge that they are unconditionally loved.' *Word of Wisdom*

Nan would say to me, 'Karen, when I die, always remember that I love you'. She repeatedly reminded me that the best thing we can gift to another human being is the knowledge that they are unconditionally loved (a great definition of evangelism, but more of that later).

Nan always wore a cross around her neck. Every Good Friday, she cried quiet tears because we caused Jesus to die for us. Easter Sunday was always a happy day. You can imagine how special it was when she took the cross from her neck and gave it to me to wear forever – the memory of my nan around my neck; the symbol of my faith, close to my heart. Wearing the cross was a great witness, too. It communicated the essence of who I was and encouraged me to good works. I would anonymously pay for random customers' meals and drinks in cafés and restaurants. Cashiers would look at me and my cross curiously as I paid the bill and left before being discovered. I didn't need to shout about my faith; the cross around my neck did it for me.

Then one day, as I picked up the cross, I felt the Holy Spirit speak to me.

'Don't put the cross around your neck.'

Surely, I had this wrong? I picked it up again, but couldn't put it on. Puzzled, I held it in my hands. Was that strong inner witness of the Holy Spirit just for today? I decided to obey His leading. The next day, the conviction from Holy Spirit not to wear the cross around my neck was as strong as ever. Surely this couldn't be right?

'No, God, you've got it wrong.' I answered, this time. 'This cross is who I am and what I do. Sometimes, the only way people know why I do those good things is because of this. It's my witness!'

But still, that silent strong conviction came to me. 'Do not wear your cross.'

I was not pleased. This really couldn't be right. I was putting myself out doing random acts of kindness for people to witness for Jesus. Demonstrating the lavish generosity of a lavish Creator. Not to mention that the cross belonged to my Nan, who loved me with so much faith and unconditional love. My precious Nan, worn close to my heart.

Grudgingly, I didn't wear it. It made no sense, but when our only choice is obedience, the fruit follows. However, I simmered with frustration. Without its witness around my neck, random acts of kindness like back-paying bills for people made little impact. God had got it wrong, I thought, and I didn't understand why.

One day, I questioned again. 'But why God, why?'

And I heard Him say:

"Too many of my people are kneeling at the foot of the Cross, and not standing at the mouth of the resurrection cave."

Did I hear correctly? It was one of those revelations which become pivotal to transformation. What did God mean by 'Too many people are kneeling at the foot of the Cross and not standing at the mouth of the resurrection cave'?

Then I saw it: Identity. Our perfect identity – not as mourners, getting it wrong and begging Jesus for forgiveness – but, in effect, pre-resurrection Christians. We are a great people, sons and daughters of the King; 'gods' (with a small 'g') in His image, dare I suggest. Small 'christs' with a small 'c', with only one God with a capital 'G' being worthy of honour and praise, sharing in our humanity, transforming us into His Divinity.

> *'"We are not stoning you for any good work," they replied, "but for blasphemy, because you, a mere man, claim to be God." Jesus answered them, "Is it not written in your Law, 'I have said you are "gods"'? If he called them 'gods,' to whom the word of God came—and Scripture cannot be set aside— what about the one*

> *whom the Father set apart as his very own and sent into the world? Why then do you accuse me of blasphemy because I said, 'I am God's Son'?"' John 10:33 -36*

Sadly, the enemy is extremely cunning in attempting to deter us from our true, powerful identity as 'gods', by virtue of our Sonship and 'Daughtership' through Jesus. Branches of the New Age movement and strands of Buddhism suggest that we are all inherently God (capital G), and have a superior identity through our union with miscellaneous forms of 'God-force.' Where the purpose of the Cross is denied or ignored and Jesus is not acknowledged as Lord, there is the danger of a false identification of self as a God, co-equal with the Lord of Heaven. Jesus left the cave after His death. His resurrection is our new life. Jesus is God inside us. His Presence within us transforms the ordinary into extraordinary, and small people into 'gods'.

Jesus will always be Lord.

> *'Jesus answered them, "Is it not written in your Law, 'I have said you are "gods"' If he called them 'gods,' to whom the word of God came—and Scripture cannot be set aside— what about the one whom the Father set apart as his very own and sent into the world?"' John 10:34-36*

Jesus uses a reference to Psalm 82:6, a prophetic word to Asaph from God, where we are described as 'gods.' The small 'g' is essential to note. There is only one Saviour, and that is Jesus.

One day, I visited a friend in a town, miles from my home. This friend had refused to believe in God, leaving me genuinely perplexed and amazed. Life as a Christian is a walking miracle, so how could she know me and not believe in Jesus? We walked together through a busy part of town, through the crowds, chatting and laughing. Then I saw her – a frail, old woman, pushing a walking frame with her head down, eyes focused on the pavement. Slowly she shuffled, step by painful step, concentrating on maintaining a momentum forward.

In the Spirit, I observed an anointing of His Presence on this old woman, who was mostly unnoticed by the rest of the world.

Mid-conversation with my atheist friend, I watched the old woman, captivated and fascinated. Suddenly, she lifted her head, looked straight at me and, in that moment, our eyes locked. She stopped and raised her bent body. Shoppers bustled about, the crowd continued its busy movement, and my idle chat didn't falter, but we held each other's gaze through it all. I smiled, according respect to this old woman of God whom I recognised in the Spirit, with no clue about who she was or where she had come from. Her eyes began to fill with tears, and, still holding my gaze, she raised herself higher, lifted her frame and inched with small, determined steps towards me.

My friend hesitated as I slowed down for the figure shuffling in our direction. The old woman shook her head and looked at me with absolute love, eyes shining. I beamed back at her.

'It's you!' The old woman announced.

Now that was a conundrum. I couldn't deny that it really was me, but who this woman was, I had no idea. And who she thought I might be, again no clues.

'Yes, it's me!' I said, smiling but slightly confused. What else could be said?

She shuffled closer, and I moved to meet her. 'But it's you!' she cried.

'Yes' I said, again, feeling slightly embarrassed and at a loss.

'It's you!' She said again. 'It's you who prays!'

I couldn't deny that, either, so I said a simple, 'Yes!'

My atheist friend was fascinated. 'Who is this, Karen?' she asked quietly, with a quick glance at the old woman.

'No idea!' I replied, as the woman closed the gap between us. She soon stood directly in front of me, let go of her frame and reached her hands to my cheeks, tears streaming from her eyes.

'But it's you who *prays*!' Then, gently gripping my cheeks, she pinched my face affectionately, shook her head, and after a second or two, turned and hobbled her way past.

I was baffled. How did she know me? How did she know I prayed? *Who was she?*

'Who *was* she, Karen?' My friend asked echoed my last question.

I really had no idea, and told this to my friend who looked at me sceptically. We went on our way.

I thought back on the encounter. I'd never met the woman before, to my knowledge, yet she knew who I was and that I prayed.

Suddenly it clicked and the revelation hit me – I wasn't wearing my cross, yet I was recognised! It was a divine set up to demonstrate that a cross around my neck didn't symbolise who I am; the person I am is already known by Heaven. The proof of my identity wasn't in that crucifix. Jesus will be made known through me, not through what I wear.

I must make clear that this was a personal lesson from God to me, not a generalisation for the millions who wear crosses daily. It was *my* message of the moment, not a general principle or rule for anyone else.

God would reinforce this lesson of 'being' with other key events in future.

> **'Our transformation is a journey toward becoming 'I am who I am', where the condition of the heart has greater significance than the industry of the hands.'** *Word of Wisdom*

Evangelism was always something I did. An activity to be performed and a somewhat painful duty which I wasn't all that good at 'doing'.

'Doing' evangelism is a bit like a visit to the dentist: a necessity, rarely looked forward to, and a mostly good feeling when it's over.

As a new Christian, I studied for years, to rehearse 'the gospel' in case I was asked. Getting the order right was imperative, getting all the words in, essential. Covering every detail in one three-minute burst became my goal. It was a relief to discover Peter's speech in Acts Chapter 3. At last, here was the gospel. What had to be said in order to convert someone, interested or not.

One day, whilst at home and decorating the living room, I realised that the shopping wasn't done, the ironing was waiting, and time was ticking away; my good intention to go cold calling on non-believers out on the streets was put aside, once again.

'I'm sorry, God,' I said sincerely. 'There just isn't time to evangelise today.'

Secretly, I was relieved. After all, God wouldn't know I didn't find evangelism pleasant or easy. Armed with a long shopping list, I drove to the supermarket. Minutes later, trolley half-full as I walked along the meat aisle, I heard God's still, small voice, like a whisper, but so powerful.

'Wake up. Look around you. This is the mission field. Open your eyes!'

The awesome realisation hit me. The mission field isn't an extraordinary place to go to or time that needs to be made. The mission field is wherever you are. It struck me like a bolt from Heaven when God simply said:

'Don't *do* evangelism; *become* evangelism.'

We can be so focused on compartmentalising our lives into activity and schedules, and miss the walk in the Spirit which is one long continuous flow, like a river.

Prayer life is another example. Have you ever noticed how some dog owners resemble their pets, or vice versa? The Pointer owner is sleek, aware, and neat. The Old English Sheep Dog owner might be scruffy and happy go lucky, with surprising talents. (The examples stop before we get to Rottweilers or Chihuahuas!) Or the married couple who begin to resemble each other, or who get ready for church dressed in similar colours, which often happens with two of my treasured friends.

It didn't take much to figure out that great men and women of God spend time with their Creator. This time in His Presence brings about change, a likeness to Jesus, and a transformation into His image.

'We become the reflection of Jesus when we have gazed at His Presence in prayer.'
Word of Wisdom

Having returned from Mission School in Africa, I decided to discipline my prayer life and spend early mornings in prayer for several hours. Not only was this unrealistic and possibly unwise from the outset, but I'm not entirely sure my motivation was right. Ambition to pray and humility are not easy companions. However, trooper that I was, I was ready for my scheduled three-hour prayer time as realistically as choosing to run the London Marathon with good intentions but no preparation.

The clock was set. The morning stretched ahead like a long expanse ahead of me, and all I had to do was focus on God and pray for three hours. Easy!?

Except that, having knelt down to pray beside my bed (my usual custom), I stretched out my arm to reach God (again quite normal) and found that I simply didn't have words. No words would come out from my mouth. I tried to speak but no sound came out.

This was tricky. What do you do for three hours on your knees, ready to pray, when nothing, not even a groan, comes out from your heart?

I opened one eye to look at God. 'What's going on?'

Was the enemy putting a barrier in my path? Was God trying to communicate something to me?

My prayer time lasted all of 10 minutes and then I got on with the rest of my day, determined that tomorrow would be a success.

It wasn't. Every day, for several days, I knelt beside my bed, ready to pour out my heart, and nothing. It was like a block on my mouth. With stubborn resolution, I knelt every morning, determined to overcome. Then it happened. Kneeling and ready, with no words, I discovered I couldn't close my eyes! My eyes stayed open, which is not the norm when adopting the traditional position of prayer.

Now this was a problem. Prayer without words, we might improvise with groans or tongues or even (radical thought) listening to and waiting on the Lord. But eyes wide open? Along with no words? Prayer became impossible. Whoever heard of praying without words, eyes wide open? It couldn't be done. My three hours were scuppered, and I had the hump with God. I was ready to grow but *He* obviously wasn't ready for me.

Sadly, these reflections were true. Someone once said development is like walking towards the horizon; it's only when you look back that you realise how far you have come!

Then it struck me like a bolt from Heaven again. God simply said:

'Don't do prayer. Become prayer.'

I suddenly recognised the freedom of living like *I am prayer* as opposed to creating a slot with God at a convenient time in the day. Again, this was a lesson for me, not for the many with a regular daily 'quiet time.' The realisation dawned that most of my waking hours are spent with my eyes open and (thankfully) my mouth shut. To become, rather than do, prayer was an incredible freedom. It was a revelation that I am alive to God everywhere. He was teaching me to walk in the Spirit!

If I am prayer, constantly communing with God, never out of His Presence, or shutting the door on my communion with Him, then the possibilities around me are infinite. He had to teach me this before I learned how to pray. This may not be everyone's journey, but it is mine. *Evangelism was no longer something I did, but something that I had become.*

A walk in the Spirit, eyes open, hearts ready, in communion with Heaven. I wonder whether we have missed out on walking step by step with the Spirit.

A passage from the Bible had always fascinated me, and if I'm honest, I wondered why Jesus had got it so wrong. Here is the account of Jesus sending out the seventy-two:

> *'After this the Lord appointed seventy-two others and sent them two by two ahead of him to every town and place where he was about to go. He told them, "The harvest is plentiful, but the workers are few. Ask the Lord of the harvest, therefore, to send out workers into his harvest field. Go! I am sending you out like lambs among wolves. Do not take a purse or bag or sandals; and do not greet anyone on the road.' Luke 10:1-4*

Jesus doesn't say 'stay in your buildings and pray for the harvest'. No! The harvest is ready and waiting for us. We often use prayer as an escape so that we don't actually 'go' as Jesus commanded. Our going is not necessarily to far flung places like Africa or the Far East, but to where we are right now. Your doorstep when a parcel is delivered. The supermarket. The hospital. School. Streets. The dentist.

Give Love A-Way

Evangelism goes where you go, because you are the best appointment Pre-Christians might have for an encounter with Jesus.

A few months back, as I arrived at Kingsland Church in Colchester, a delivery driver approached carrying a large box. He was limping. What would Love do as he stood by the elevator doors? I had seen him; which is the first challenge. We can be so focused on task and our own agenda, failing to spot the obvious one in front of us. Love looks like action.

In her books, Heidi Baker (IRIS Global Ministries) teaches us to 'stop for the one'. Stop for the one in front of us. Make love count. The delivery man was the one in front of me.

'Excuse me,' I said, 'I work here. Can I take that parcel to reception for you? Should save you some time!'

He looked up. 'Please. My leg is in agony.' he replied. 'Every now and again, it plays up for a few months. It's really hurting today and I'm struggling to walk.'

My heart sank.

> *'Heal the sick, raise the dead, cleanse those who have leprosy, drive out demons. Freely you have received; freely give.' Matthew 10:8*

To pray for or heal the sick, which is what Jesus commands, should be easy to obey. If anyone mentions sickness, I will ask for permission to pray, based on this command. With very little joy, I must add, as my rate of healing success seems to be low. But the results are not mine. They belong to God. It's my job to be relentlessly obedient and look like love. This poor delivery driver was going to have me pray for his healing and probably walk away in as much pain as when he arrived. Oh, me of little faith.

'Where is the pain?' I asked.

He explained that his calf muscle would tighten for periods of time, causing excruciating pain.

'I am a Christian.' I explained. 'I believe Jesus heals today, just as He did when He walked on the planet. Can I pray for your leg to be healed?'

The next blow was to hear him say yes.

Oh no. I groaned inwardly. Have you ever had that feeling?

I asked for permission to place my hand on his lower leg. That was a mistake, as he should have laid his own hand on his leg. However, God honours our stepping out, even when we make mistakes.

I spoke to his leg in the authority of Jesus. 'Leg pain, go, in Jesus name. Muscles, relax. Calf, work perfectly.' I ordered. 'Lord, bless this leg to work perfectly and without pain.'

Next, I checked back in with him. 'How are you doing? How is the pain now? Check out your leg.'

'Much better,' he said, testing out his leg by stretching and walking.

'Try and walk a little to see how it feels,' I said. The activation of faith, as demonstrated by Jesus in the Gospels, will often lead to healing. He walked tentatively, with less of a limp. However, I took his 'much better' to mean 'it's just the same but I'm going to protect you from the truth'.

We mustn't let our lack of faith stop us. God can act despite our unbelief; we must be obedient to the Word and see what He does.

Heartened, the delivery driver told me his grandmother was a Pentecostal believer who travelled the world for Jesus and loved the Holy Spirit.

(Please note that at no stage had I asked the driver for his own spiritual status. Christian or not, he deserved the same response.)

As he walked away, I received a word of knowledge which I quickly slipped in. 'You feel like you're chasing your tail trying to earn money to keep your family. It feels like a treadmill you can't escape.'

He turned around. 'That's true. I do.'

'Your grandmother had her priorities right. She put Jesus first. Jesus said if you seek first His Kingdom and His righteousness, everything else must follow. It's worth getting your priorities right, eh?'

'That's true,' he said.

'And one last thing,' I added, aware that the poor guy was probably up against time pressures. 'I see a word written on your life. You have the gift of preaching. It's your destiny to preach.'

Now this was a risk. At this stage, I have no way of reliably knowing whether he is a Christian. His grandmother's heritage might not be his own. His story needed to be his own.

He looked at me strangely. 'I never told you my name?' he replied, half as a question.

(Error number two. Karen, always ask the person their name before ministering. Names are important and create relationship.)

I shook my head. 'No. What is it?'

'My grandmother prayed for me right from birth. In fact, she had such a strong sense of God's calling on my life that she gave me a preacher's name. My name is...' (He gave me a well-known 19th Century preacher's name!)

What a memorable encounter. Looking like love, in the place where you are.

In the Luke 10 Scripture, Jesus says to pray for the workers to be sent out; a far greater challenge than bringing in the harvest. But here's the gripe, friends. Here's my gripe. Why did Jesus tell the disciples not to greet anyone on the road? It made no sense. What a missed opportunity for evangelism! Surely the road is our best chance as we move from place to place? When I am in town, and switched on, I often catch people's eyes, smile and engage.

But here's the point.

Jesus gave His disciples permission to switch off because they were always with Him. For us, in this 21st Century world, it's mostly the opposite. Our focus can largely become convoluted by the world, its schedules and drive toward pressure, time management, juggling and responsibility. With our awareness switched off from Him, our attention largely on our own needs and agendas, we miss the walk in the Spirit that is our post-resurrection heritage and starting point.

Jesus gave the disciples the permission to switch off on the road and rest because they were always spiritually switched on. For us Christians today, it's often the opposite.

As Lord of the harvest, it's notable that Jesus sent out His disciples, in twos, to every place that He was **about** to go. From sowing these seeds, Jesus would reap the harvest. How comforting to know that we are simply seed sowers in God's great rescue plan. We are sowers of seed. When our heart's intention is to look like love with every person we encounter, we sow seed for the Kingdom that can be watered by our Heavenly Father and reaped by Jesus. Conversion was never our responsibility; it is always His. Persuasion belongs to the Lord.

Evangelism is rarely using the gospel to confront Pre-Christians. Sometimes I have seen Romans 1:16 used as an excuse for repelling Pre-Christians with a judgemental harshness that creates barriers and walls where none need exist.

> 'For I am not ashamed of the gospel, because it is
> the power of God that brings salvation to everyone
> who believes: first to the Jew, then to the Gentile.'
> Romans 1:16

Of course, we are not ashamed of the gospel. Understanding that the gospel is love in its purest form, shown to us and others when we didn't deserve it, makes our job as lovers of God and lovers of others, such a pleasure. And so easy, in the Spirit.

The gospel shared without love probably isn't the gospel. It's probably judgement.

The revelation hit me one day as I read the Sermon on the Mount, Jesus' own 'manifesto' for God-like living. How could I possibly fulfil, remember, practice, and obey all these commands? Do them correctly and on time? Get them right?

The Beatitudes. For years I misread and pronounced them as 'Beauty-tudes', and so they are. Beauty attitudes. The 'Be'-attitudes. Not the 'Do'-attitudes.

Being. Becoming. Growing. A journey of becoming.

Being so filled and permeated by the Spirit that our old flesh-self diminishes and the new Spirit-filled self-increases.

The revelation hit me, that the Spirit transforms us into Be-ings who outflow from the inflow. By their fruit they shall be known. Don't *do* the sermon on the mount i.e., try hard, persist and sacrifice. Allow yourself to be so transformed by the Spirit that the outflow, the natural outcome from your being, is the fulfilment of love. In other words, it is living the gospel. We *become* the sermon on the mount through intimacy with the Holy Spirit. Having more love for others and putting God above every other desire in your life. Fruit.

Often, people don't feel good enough for church. Somehow, the Christian life has become about obeying the rules and good living. We must get back in touch with the Spirit. In that place with Him is freedom and life. The stereotypical Christian is portrayed in today's media by religious stereotypes as being good, like the Vicar of Dibley (an English comedy on TV with a nice but ineffectual church leader), insipid, woolly, or out of touch. Essentially, they are powerless.

We find our Superheroes in cartoons and comics, not realising that we are this planet's superheroes; filled with power, filled with Jesus.

Points to reflect on:

- We are human 'beings', and not human 'doings.'
- The Beatitudes in Matthew are 'Be'-attitudes, and not 'Do'-attitudes.
- This journey into the Spirit and fellowship with Him is a flow of being, the outflow from which is our doing. Being precedes doing.
- Get the 'being' right and the 'doing' flows from there.
- The inflow of the Spirit determines the outflow from our lives. We overflow.
- We are constantly filled.
- When describing Himself, God never said: 'I am what I do'. Nor did He say; 'I do what I am.' He said that the name for Himself is the 'I AM WHO I AM.' This is also our journey, a journey of becoming.

Talk with and listen to the Spirit of the Father, the Spirit of Jesus: The Holy Spirit.

CHAPTER 2 – INTIMACY WITH THE HOLY SPIRIT

"And if I go and prepare a place for you, I will come back and take you to be with me that you also may be where I am." John 14:3

Who is He Really?

A Scripture kept me puzzled for weeks:

"'But very truly I tell you, it is for your good that I am going away. Unless I go away, the Advocate will not come to you; but if I go, I will send him to you.'" John 16:7

Why did Jesus have to go away before the Holy Spirit was released on earth? I wanted to know what it was about the body of Jesus that meant He had to depart for the Spirit to come. During that period of questioning and curiosity, I got my answer from an unexpected source.

As part of the Healing on the Streets team in Chelmsford, it was my role to engage with passers-by and ask whether they needed healing in their body. We would then invite the person to sit on a chair, and two team members would pray. Amazing. We saw wonderful testimonies from our times in Chelmsford's market square.

The biggest challenge was finding people interested, brave or trusting enough to take a seat. I struggled in the beginning, too shy and hesitant to step out. But then I watched my friend Barbara lead a continual stream of people to those seats. I had a competitive streak at the time (a sort of holy or, rather, unholy jealousy) – Barbara was getting more people than me and I wanted a continual stream of people, too.

Barbara seemed to do it just by being friendly and smiling. It wasn't rocket science! At best, I was probably giving off, 'I'm sorry for entering your world when you're obviously extremely busy' or 'this isn't something a reasonable person would attempt' vibes. At worst, I wished the three hours would go by quickly so I could get home and enjoy the rest of my Saturday.

And so, in for the penny and pound, I followed Barbara's example and became bold and friendly. Instead of waiting for someone to show interest, I viewed everyone as an opportunity to offer prayer.

Soon, I, too, was leading a stream of people to the seats for healing. Then I met Victor.

Victor was carrying a six-pack of cheese and onion crisps, eating one pack as he walked. Victor looked like an old sailor in a cream, thick, woollen polo neck jumper and blue jeans. He had an appealing charm about him.

I approached him. 'Excuse me, Sir. May I have a crisp?' The apostle Paul said he became all things to all men to win some for Christ. Plus, I hadn't had lunch!

He offered me a crisp, then retracted it and gave me a whole bag. His eyes were bright blue and clear; his hair white and neat.

Ok, I thought, he's offered me crisps. Can I engage him in a spiritual conversation? I was in fully-primed evangelism mode: Watch out, world! Stealth evangelism attack about to commence. Woman with an agenda, at the ready with all the answers, probably not listening. Not looking like love.

'Thank you for the crisps. My name is Karen, may I ask yours?'

We crunched crisps companionably.

'And Vic,' I said, after his update, 'I'm never going to see you again, so can I ask you a question?'

It helps to have a one-liner ready to open up a conversation. This one often works well for me since people feel more secure about a no-strings-attached conversation.

He looked at me curiously (people often do).

'Do you believe in God?' I usually start at first base and build from there. If the answer is no, I might say, 'and why don't you believe?' Not in a punitive or judgemental way, but in a genuine attempt to understand their motivation for unbelief. Tragedy is often behind unbelief, for example; 'Why did God let my loved one die?'

'What do you mean by believe?' Vic replied.

'Do you believe in God?' I countered, slightly flummoxed. Vic had thrown down the gauntlet.

His head angled to one side, Vic said, 'Belief can mean many things. Do you mean, am I spiritual?'

'Yes.'

For the next ten minutes, Vic asked me challenging and searching questions like: What is God? Did God create evil? Who created darkness and for what purpose? etc.

I was confused. Supposedly in evangelism mode, here I was being asked searching and deep questions. Not for answers, as Vic already seemed to know each Scripture-based answer.

Irritatingly, after every answer, he smiled and responded to my replies with 'correct!'.

Who was this man? I began to suspect all wasn't as it seemed.

And then the absolutely clinch question, from Vic to me. 'What happened to Jesus' body after He died?'

Aha! Got him! I thought. Still in that wretched evangelism mode, trying to win a non-existent battle. How unlike Jesus evangelism can look.

'Well, He came back in His body. We know this because Thomas and the other disciples saw and touched His wounds. He then took His body into the sky when He disappeared from the disciples' view.'

'Correct,' countered Vic, smiling again.

I stared in puzzled wonder, anticipating an answer to the question I had carried for weeks.

'Jesus had to take His body with Him after the resurrection in order to release His Spirit to complete the work on earth before His return.' Vic explained.

The penny dropped! Only one Jesus, prior to His resurrection, limited to just one physical body!

We are the body of Jesus on earth today! If Jesus arrived in the flesh in Manchester at 6pm tonight, no doubt the roads and airports across the UK would be clogged with believers trying to meet their Lord, not least unbelievers seeking healing and freedom, given Jesus' track record in the New Testament.

And so now we have the Spirit of Jesus with us. The exact representation of His being in Spirit form, within, upon and around us; equipping us to be Jesus on this planet today! With the breath of God in us, we go from ordinary to extraordinary believers. *We are Jesus' hands, His feet, His mouth, His heart, His body, on this planet, here today.*

Who do we see when we look at Jesus?

> *'Jesus answered: "Don't you know me, Philip, even after I have been among you such a long time? Anyone who has seen me has seen the Father. How can you say, 'Show us the Father'? Don't you believe that I am in the Father, and that the Father is in me? The words I say to you I do not speak on my*

> own authority. Rather, it is the Father, living in me, who is doing
> his work. Believe me when I say that I am in the Father and the
> Father is in me; or at least believe on the evidence of the works
> themselves.' John 14:9-11

When we look at Jesus, we see the Father.

> "For I will pour water on the thirsty land,
> and streams on the dry ground;
> I will pour out my Spirit on your offspring,
> and my blessing on your descendants." Isaiah 44:3

Who do we see if we put flesh on the Spirit?

> "And afterward, I will pour out my Spirit on all people.
> Your sons and daughters will prophesy, your old men will dream
> dreams, your young men will see visions. Even on my
> servants, both men and women,
> I will pour out my Spirit in those days." Joel 2:28-29

'My Spirit...' says the Lord. Not *the* Spirit. Not some nameless ethereal wisp of air, devoid of personality or form. 'My Spirit,' The Spirit of Jesus.

It naturally follows, therefore, that if you put flesh on the Holy Spirit, we see Jesus!

When we look at Jesus, who do we see? The Father, Jesus said. If you have seen me then you have seen the Father, He told His disciples.

> 'Hear, O Israel: The LORD our God, the LORD is one.
> Love the LORD your God with all your heart and with all
> your soul and with all your strength. These commandments
> that I give you today are to be on your hearts. Impress
> them on your children. Talk about them when you sit at
> home and when you walk along the road, when you lie
> down and when you get up. Tie them as symbols on your
> hands and bind them on your foreheads. Write them on the

> *doorframes of your houses and on your gates.'*
> Deuteronomy 6:4-9

One God in three forms. Father, Son, Spirit.

And yet we have mostly relegated the Holy Spirit from His rightful role as God, to the role of a subservient servant. We simply don't know Him. We need relationship, the fellowship Paul describes in the grace we say so often to each other:

> *'May the grace of the Lord Jesus Christ, and the love of God, and the fellowship of the Holy Spirit be with you all.'*
> 2 Corinthians 13:14

Fellowship. Relationship; conferring with, listening and speaking to, asking and hearing from our teacher, comforter, advocate and guide.

The Holy Spirit Connects us to Jesus

A few years back, while in worship, I had a waking or mind vision (I'm not entirely what it is called). I went in my thoughts to a place where a scene began to emerge. It was so real, that even now, tears fill my eyes as I write because the time in my memory is so vivid.

It was a desert with intense heat and a strong wind blowing hot on my face. Mountains lay some distance ahead, but the place was empty and arid. A dust-coloured brown could be seen for endless miles. Even the mountains ahead were dust brown.

Some metres ahead stood Jesus, with His back to me. He stood, leaning into the strong wind, emanating joy, a sense of energy and anticipation as though He wanted to stride ahead. His cloak blew back in the wind, and His hair, down to His waist, flowed back too.

I could only stare.

He half-turned and extended a hand back towards me, presumably to accompany Him forward. But I couldn't do it. Even though everything inside me wanted to, I couldn't move towards His extended hand. And here this vision stayed and played out week after week in the time of worship at church. Nothing could move me to take His hand. It was desperate and frustrating, but I simply didn't have a solution.

One day, I decided to make it happen. Tears streamed down my face, but I was determined to bridge that gap and force myself to take His hand. What was separating me from oneness with Jesus? Sin? My will? I had to take His outstretched hand. I tried so hard to get to Him, but was still unable.

Suddenly, I forced myself closer and took His hand. In that moment, the Holy Spirit somehow took me and instead of holding Jesus' hand, I was actually transposed *inside* Jesus! I leaned into the wind, facing the mountains with the heat of the wind on my face. Somehow, I was IN Jesus, and Jesus was IN me. Could this be? That I was in Jesus and Jesus was in me? I was no longer a follower of Jesus, taken by His hand. I was 'in Christ', and Christ was now inside of me.

My months of effort in trying to reach and go with Jesus had failed. The Holy Spirit was the Divine Vehicle, transposing my life into Jesus and Jesus' life into mine. My struggle ceased to be about trying hard, and desire. I 'became', having been spiritually transposed into oneness with Jesus because of and by the Holy Spirit.

I was no longer just a 'follower' of Jesus; I was actually one with Him, through the Spirit. That is our journey here on this planet.

> *" Don't you believe that I am in the Father, and that the Father is in me?"' John 14:10*

There is a oneness with God that comes through the Spirit, or *because* of the Spirit.

> *"' I will not leave you as orphans; I will come to you. Before long, the world will not see me anymore, but you will see me. Because I live, you also will live. On that day you will realize that I am in my Father, and you are in me, and I am in you.'" John 14:18-20*

The disciples, before the coming of the Spirit, intensely focus on *following*. Yet after being filled with the Spirit, their works are the outflow of the inflow. In the Old Testament times, God actively directed His people; speaking to, advising, guiding, and leading them through external means like clouds, fire. and one-to-one chats with heroes of faith. We are all now heroes of the faith, with God in us. It is so powerful. God within, directing, inspiring, energizing and leading us. We simply have to come awake and discover the possibility and purpose of our God within us; Immanuel.

Talk with and listen to the Spirit of the Father, the Spirit of Jesus: The Holy Spirit.

CHAPTER 3 – IRIS HARVEST MISSION SCHOOL 21

Dancing with the Holy Spirit

'As iron sharpens iron, so one person sharpens another.'
Proverbs 27:17

There I was in South Africa, in a wooden hut with three other women, cold and huddled in my sleeping bag on a straw mattress. My application had been accepted along with over 250 other students from over 35 nations. I had drawn the long straw, and honour of sleeping in the hut on a straw bed because I was an older woman. Unlike the other students who camped on a sloped field with six portable toilets and outdoor showers. It was frigid. Somehow, we hadn't imagined cold in Africa, but the temperature dropped at night and we awoke to a cold mist and thick sparkling dew on the open field, dotted with tiny tents of all colours. Welcome to Mission School!

Three months stretched ahead with worship, international teachers, practical tasks and community living. Sometimes with water, sometimes without. Sometimes with electricity, and sometimes not. Poisonous red and black frogs collected in the toilet cistern and shared our bathroom space. Preparation for mission?

Rachel (name changed for the purposes of this book) and I shared a hut. She was (and is) a 'full on', wonderful, beautiful, African-American extravert New Yorker that Jesus rescued from addiction to drugs and other horrors on the streets of New York. A powerful woman of God, Rachel was loud. I loved her, as did the whole camp. She stood out, because of her bold communication and her full-on dedication to Jesus. He is her world.

Give Love A-Way

I soon discovered that Rachel had an annoying problem. At between 5.30-6.00 a.m. every morning, she needed the toilet. Have you noticed how, whenever you're trying not to be heard, loud things seem to happen? That is how it was with Rachel. Every morning, with rustling movements, the door opened and was left ajar, as Rachel disappeared to the toilet. Everyone else woke up, and went back to sleep. Except Rachel didn't return to the hut. *Where did she go?*

As you do, one morning, I decided to go after her. Curiosity or suspicion? I like to think it was curiosity.

Semi quiet again, Rachel got up and out she went at 5.45am. I slipped a coat over my night clothes, fixed on my shoes and squeezed out from the hut's front door. Down the field, Rachel was making her way to the portable toilets. So far so good. I wandered down, too. Then the dilemma. I couldn't loiter outside the toilets, so I found an empty cubicle and utilised the moment.

Out came Rachel, carrying something under her arm. She detoured across the field to a quiet space where there was the large worship tent, empty under the frozen South African sky. Rachel pulled up a chair behind the space and sat down in the freezing morning air where breath collected like cloud as you breathed out. She placed her Bible on her lap and began to pray. She was ready for God.

Sheepishly, I returned to the hut and quickly got back into my sleeping bag. She was spending time with God at a time when I was usually sleeping. It nagged at me. Rachel was on fire for God; I was happy to sleep. The benefits of waking up early and giving the first fruits of the day to God were so obvious.

The decision was made. I would get up early to spend time alone with God. No mean feat in a field in South Africa housing 250 students and staff. At 5.45 a.m. I awoke, got up in the darkness, all prepared with coat, shoes and Bible. I fumbled around and left the hut. Amazingly, before Rachel was up.

I found a place in the field away from Rachel's space and prepared to meet with God. It was barely light and still very cold. The dew wet my training shoes and I shivered in the semi darkness. What would happen next, I wondered?

Rachel, having discovered me in the field, obviously had the same thoughts as me. She resolved to get up at 5.30 a.m. the next morning. This prompted me (yes, it's ridiculous!) to get up at 5.15 a.m. the following day.

The luxury of time and space, and the freedom to just *be* at that time, in what, by 9 a.m., would become a camp overrun with people, was a wonder. I looked across at Rachel in her space, and she looked at me, both of us looking ready to leave our places in the field. Hot coffee would be ready at 8 a.m. We walked back to the canteen to warm ourselves and get some breakfast.

'We're both ready at a similar time in the morning.' Rachel said. 'Why don't we go out together?'

'Great plan!'

This is exactly what we did, at 5 a.m. and sometimes as early as 4.30 a.m. each morning, we quietly gathered our things and took ourselves to our own space in the field to meet with God. Rachel's lifestyle taught me how to pursue God and live devoted to Jesus.

Soon we became best buddies. My name would be called from various parts of the camp. 'Karen! Where's my bestie?'

Rachel did have another annoying habit – her boldness. I say this with some irony, as the problem didn't belong to Rachel. (Funny how we can project blame onto others for our own inadequacies.) I didn't have her level of boldness. I knew I was lacking. I was just so British; so contained!

> **'The Presence of God will always bring transformation.'** *Word of Wisdom*

Speakers from all over the world came to Harvest School; International speakers and leaders dedicated to teaching, facilitating growth, and bringing us into the Presence of God.

Rachel would make herself known to these leaders and would ask them for prophetic words, prayers of blessing and impartation. Each time she encountered a leader, she journaled the outcome and shared the journal's content with me. A part of me admired Rachel, wanting the same, but without the cost of being bold enough to ask.

We were an incongruent pair. Rachel, loudly extravert, fearless and dynamic; and me so British, reserved and quiet. Yet, we matched in the Spirit. Rachel, a full-on leader, me, under the radar, both equally aware of the Holy Spirit's power and purpose. Perfect how God uses our personality to suit His purposes. I could never be Rachel, and she could never be me, and it didn't matter that we were different. We were each perfectly equipped for our own calling.

> **'Your personality is built perfectly for His purposes.'** *Word of Wisdom*

Around the third week on camp, there was a team with us from Catch the Fire church in Toronto. At midday, after a morning teaching session for the whole school, I noticed one of the Toronto team standing on the periphery of the meeting tent, watching as everyone chatted or dispersed for lunch. She was slight, with remarkable eyes. Her eyes, even from a distance, were amazing. I realised this woman had the gift of the seer. I had to meet her. I had this gift too, and connecting with her might lead to learning more about it. This was my time! Perhaps she might even give me a prophetic word?

Having learned from Rachel's confidence not to waste an opportunity, I went over to the woman. The only thing was, the moment's excitement overrode my walk in the Spirit. I approached her very much in the flesh, not in the Spirit. Wisdom was woefully, painfully and obviously absent!

'Hello! My name is Karen!' I announced, extending a hand. 'I saw you from the other side of the room and noticed that you have a seeing gift. I have a seeing gift too!' (Not a great start.)

We shook hands, and she looked at me wordlessly, which propelled me into another gushing advance:

'I'm so pleased to meet you. I haven't met another seer before!'

Hardly any expression crossed her face as she looked at me. Then she said slowly and carefully, 'The same Spirit, who raised Jesus from the dead, is in you.'

Interesting. I thought.

'Thanks. I know!' I enthused. 'Isn't that great news!'

She looked hard and intently at me. 'The same Spirit, who raised Jesus from the dead, *is in you.*'

Hmm. Curious. Repeating the same thing, with slightly different emphasis on words. Was I meant to get some sort of message?

'Yes, isn't that great!' I replied, suddenly thinking this wasn't going at all well. A speedy exit looked appealing.

For a third time, she said slowly and pointedly, 'The same Spirit, who raised Jesus from the dead, is in you.' Only, this time, she leaned in close, peered at me from her lion-like eyes, and added: 'And the Holy Spirit wants a relationship with you.'

Now she had my attention. The Holy Spirit wanted a relationship? With me? How dare she say that? Didn't she know that I had been baptised in the Spirit over 30 years ago? Was she aware that I spoke in tongues? The Holy Spirit wanted a relationship with me, a believer of over 30 years? How could she be so wrong?

Suddenly, I wasn't impressed with her. She clearly wasn't a seer after all, since she got it so horribly wrong. Plus, I didn't get my prophetic word!

'Erm, yes. That's great. Thanks for your time.' I backed away and left as quickly as I could, disgruntled and cross.

How could that go so wrong? I seethed. The Holy Spirit wanted a relationship with me? A Spirit-filled, Bible-believing believer baptised in water and Spirit? I had been on several missions, was once a church leader, committed to following Jesus? What did she mean?

But did I have a relationship with the Holy Spirit? I rarely, if ever, spoke directly to Him. Strangely enough, John 14, 15, 16, had drawn my attention for weeks. I poured over each line, hungry to know who, why and what the Spirit is, and what the answers to these questions might mean. Rachel was studying the same passages.

Was a relationship with the Spirit even permissible? Is it heresy to talk with the Spirit of Jesus? Can we know Him in the same way we know the Father and Jesus? How many of us can honestly say we have an intimate relationship with the Holy Spirit? Not me. What did it mean?

Thankfully, He set about teaching me.

'To follow the leading of the Spirit is to follow the leading of Jesus.' *Word of Wisdom*

Those cold early mornings in South Africa are memorable. Rachel and I were intent on pursuing the Lord and laying our lives open to His transforming Presence. It wasn't a choice. It was 'deep calling to deep.'

I had been into this journey of becoming for some time now. God had challenged me not to 'do' but to 'be' evangelism. This wasn't switch on, switch off. This was flow in the Spirit. And as I stood, holding my breath early that morning in the dew-cloaked field, I had absolutely nothing to give. There I was, in the middle of a field, just God and me.

It was there I sensed the leading of the Spirit to dance with Him. Is that strange? We have a beautiful love poem, Song of Songs leading with 'Let Him kiss me with the kisses of His mouth[1].' God desires intimacy.

The Holy Spirit would teach me to dance. Not free flow, oh no. I am after all British. But each day, as I stood, He added a new step, as He taught me the beginnings of a perfect waltz like dance.

Humming the same tune every morning, I prophetically enacted putting my hand in His, sensing His arms around me (God made man in His own image. It figures that the Holy Spirit can have arms, too).

At first, the moves were stilted, self-conscious, awkward, and slightly wary. Had I lost my senses? But every day, in the freezing cold field, another move was added to 'the dance', until I 'rested my cheek' on His shoulder and followed His moves. A flow with the Spirit.

In his letter to the Galatians, Paul encourages the followers to 'walk by the Spirit' (Galatians 5:16). This has to be a conscious awareness of walking with Him. It is intimacy and knowing that the Spirit is with us at all times.

> *'But I say, walk by the Spirit, and you will not gratify the desires of the flesh.' Galatians 5:16*

Later, in verse 25 of Galatians 5, Paul says;

> *'If we live by the Spirit, let us also keep in step with the Spirit.'*

One of my most awkward memories in life was the call to dance the first waltz at a friend's wedding. As Chief Bridesmaid, the Best Man and I, awkward, embarrassed and unprepared, were called forward to stand in the centre of the dance floor. Neither of us had a clue, but, two difficult minutes of vague and terrible shuffling backwards and forwards later, having stepped on each other's toes, we were rescued by the other guests who took to the dance floor and danced the waltz properly. How could I do what I had not been taught?

Yet, here I was, dancing with the Spirit in South Africa, following His lead.

---

[1]Song of Songs 1:2

Each day, I sensed a new movement in the dance that the Holy Spirit began to teach me. I hummed the same waltz-like tune to a pop song whose lyrics I didn't fully recognise, but now know to be Katie Melua's *'When You Taught Me How to Dance.'* It became my prayer as I opened my heart and allowed the Holy Spirit to lead me.

The first steps of the dance were initially stilted, awkward and difficult. As I connected with Him, the awareness that my life could never be the same again grew. Relationship with the Spirit, a lifelong journey of discovery, had begun. There is so much more. On those cold, quiet mornings in the field at Harvest School, South Africa, a sanctified God imagination developed and grew as time progressed, allowing God to use my mind.

It's so important to know that we have the mind of Christ.

> *'What we have received is not the spirit of the world, but the Spirit who is from God, so that we may understand what God has freely given us. This is what we speak, not in words taught us by human wisdom but in words taught by the Spirit, explaining spiritual realities with Spirit-taught words. The person without the Spirit does not accept the things that come from the Spirit of God but considers them foolishness, and cannot understand them because they are discerned only through the Spirit. The person with the Spirit makes judgments about all things, but such a person is not subject to merely human judgments, for, "Who has known the mind of the Lord so as to instruct him?"*
>
> *But we have the mind of Christ.' 1 Corinthians 2:12-16*

This mind allows me to engage with God in my thoughts and internal vision. It allows God to engage with me. God says to Jeremiah;

> *"Call to me and I will answer you and tell you great and unsearchable things you do not know."' Jeremiah 33:3*

For weeks, several different people (unbeknownst to each other) kept telling me, 'God is calling you to the throne.' 'He's taking you to the throne.' Their words meant nothing to me. I had no concept of the throne and no real desire to go there. How could I know what it meant?

One day, in the silence of the field, I began to 'see', in my mind's eye, crowds of warrior-angels on white horses. Hundreds of thousands of them, ready for battle. The horses jostled and occasionally reared with the angels on their backs. I stood in their midst, slightly perplexed, feeling out of place, with no idea what to do. It took some time for me to walk beyond this 'scene' and up to what I knew to be another level.

On this next level, past the warrior angels, sat the Father on His throne. He was waiting for me to draw close to Him. In fact, to sit on His lap like a child. Again, I was largely clueless. What should I do at this stage? I had no concept of familiarity, let alone intimacy, with the Father. In my mind, I stared at this figure as He looked at me, waiting for my approach, knowing He wanted me close, to sit with Him and to feel His love, but I just couldn't.

It took weeks of bravery to slowly climb up on that throne, and sit with the Father in my mind's sight. Trust was developing, and His patience gave me the confidence to approach Him. Every fresh day, the vision began with me surrounded by warrior angels, ready for instruction. Moving awkwardly past them, I approached the throne and climbed onto the Father's lap, eventually able to rest my head on His chest, listening to His heart beat. I had the sense of His love and pleasure, along with an awareness of His understanding of where I was placed, neither pushing nor rushing me.

One day, Father encouraged me off from His lap, sent me further on the journey, and showed me Moses. Father told me that Moses had the most intimate relationship with Him of everyone in the Bible. After some weeks, He showed me Elijah, whom Father said had engaged with the power of God more than any other figure in the Bible (I believe Jesus, as God, didn't figure in this human line-up). There is so much to learn from Moses and Elijah, the two great prophets and heroes of faith whose stories we find in the Old Testament.

An Interpretation

Father showed me that He commands the warring angels, and these warrior angels can be dispatched by Him all over the Earth in this Heavenly battle between forces of good and evil. These warrior hosts work on our behalf.

He showed me that the first level of prayer is petitionary prayer, or asking the Father to intervene in situations with the angelic realms. The angelic realms are at my disposal, at His command. We take our concerns and cares to the Father and He commands His angels concerning us. I don't instruct the angelic realms. We petition the Father in the battle. We pour out our hearts to Him.

I had the sense that these angels are ready to be deployed all over the world. No concern is too much for the Father. He is always ready, as are His army Hosts.

> *'For he will command his angels concerning you to guard you in all your ways;'* Psalm 91:11

At the end of this emerging vision (it still evolves to this day) I jump from the edge of a cliff into what feels like a bottomless void. To jump is a risk, as I know I will fall into the 'void'. It involves a feeling of trepidation and vulnerability. I stand on the 'cliff edge', Jesus takes my hand, and we jump in together. My first sensation is that we are falling deeper, but then, as Jesus holds my hand, we are flying together.

And in this mental image, I realise that I haven't jumped into an eternal void, but into the heart of the Holy Spirit. The trepidation and feeling of vulnerability come from holding on to the self, or to the ego or flesh, we might say. But to surrender oneself in complete trust means that fear cannot have a hold on us.

There are places to go and people to see in this world as we accompany Jesus, in the heart of the Spirit.

God is transforming our inner landscape through new understanding and experience. It is only safe because we are in Him, and He is in us. God is, after all, the first, greatest and best Psychologist known to man!

God Will Restore Your Past

The final amazing act of God at Harvest School happened when the staff team left travelled to Kruger Safari Park in South Africa for a weekend away.

I had gone to Harvest School in a broken state, having recently returned to church fellowship after 17 years of doing Christianity alone. I had retired from church 'injured', and still wasn't all that comfortable around large groups of Christians. My primary purpose in attending the school was to seek God; so I kept my head down at Harvest School, maintained a low profile and tried to blend in to the background. I mostly felt like an observer looking in.

To my complete surprise, I was left in charge all the women at Harvest School while the leaders were away. A great guy called Steve looked after the smaller group of guys. What could possibly go wrong?

The morning the leaders left, an acute, vomiting diarrhoea-type virus struck the camp. Within hours, around 40 people had become violently unwell. It had spread quickly through a dorm of 80 women, and a few people lay on bedding outside the dorms, in walking distance of the few toilet cubicles in the camp. To cut a long story short, several emergencies required on-the-spot resolutions and quick decisions. I found myself in a position where saying 'Yes' became the best solution.

The lack of facilities and potential contamination were immediate issues as sick people packed into minimal toilet spaces. People came to me with suggestions, volunteering to solve issues as they arose.

'Shall I get a team together to clean toilets with disinfectant?'
'Yes.' I replied,
'Shall I segregate the toilets and showers into sick and healthy sections?'

'Yes.'
'Can we take fresh water to people who can't move from their beds?'
'Yes.'
'Can we use the washing machines to wash bedding and clothes for the sick?'
'Yes.'

The issues seemed endless. All day long, medical staff cared for several more seriously unwell people. Casualties of the virus increased as the day progressed. I visited the sick and pitched in to clean toilets, floors and showers. The situation lasted for three days, yet, peace reigned in the camp the whole time. The entire community remained focused on serving each other in practical love and service.

For all my hiding, God suddenly elevated me to a leadership role and determined that I would succeed. I may have looked like an efficient leader, but all I really did was look like love and say 'yes' in challenging circumstances. I tried persuading the returned leaders that, for three days, I had simply said yes to the real servants who had ideas and took these ideas on board, and those who created teams to resolve problems.

Why is this relevant? Because your past is not an obstacle to your future success. Your future success is found in putting God first and seeking Him above all things. He is truly great.

I learned a huge amount that weekend.

'Legalism looks like 'no', but grace looks like "yes".' *Word of Wisdom*

I'm not surprised that all God's promises are 'yes' and 'amen'. We are at our best in leadership when we look like love, not control.

'Control is power used without love.' *Word of Wisdom*

From this experience in South Africa, I learned that God will use our past for Kingdom victory and glory when we surrender it to Him. From a position of hiding, hurt and woundedness, God gave me leadership and healing.

Talk with and listen to the Spirit of the Father, the Spirit of Jesus: The Holy Spirit.

CHAPTER 4 – THREE WAYS OF BEING

> *'He said to them: "It is not for you to know the times or dates the Father has set by his own authority. But you will receive power when the Holy Spirit comes on you; and you will be my witnesses in Jerusalem, and in all Judea and Samaria, and to the ends of the earth."'*
> Acts 1:7-8

Knowing Who You Really Are

'Too many of my people are kneeling at the foot of the Cross, and not standing at the mouth of the resurrection cave.'

> *'On the evening of that first day of the week, when the disciples were together, with the doors locked for fear of the Jewish leaders, Jesus came and stood among them and said, "Peace be with you!" After he said this, he showed them his hands and side. The disciples were overjoyed when they saw the Lord. Again, Jesus said, "Peace be with you! As the Father has sent me, I am sending you." And with that he breathed on them and said, "Receive the Holy Spirit. If you forgive anyone's sins, their sins are forgiven; if you do not forgive them, they are not forgiven."' John 20:19-23*

Did you ever wonder where the Power is now? That power and the outcomes demonstrated daily in Jesus and His followers' lives across the New Testament? Why don't we have more miracles, testimonies of healing and hunger for reaching out to others?

The Bible appears to identify three different positions from which we exist in our Christian lives: An Old Testament lifestyle, the Pre-Pentecost life found in the Gospels, and the Post-Pentecost or Holy Spirit-focused living.

Understanding the differences between each is fundamental to knowing and living out the true identity inherited for us by Jesus.

This teaching arose when God challenged my understanding of Kingdom position and identity by contrasting 'kneeling at the foot of the Cross' with 'standing at the mouth of the resurrection cave'. This teaching is so dangerous that revelation of its truth may mean that life and church experience can never be the same. The differences are so subtle, and yet, so potent to our future Christian experience.

When you're invited to a three-course meal, stopping with the starter won't suffice. But if you didn't know the starter wasn't the full meal, you might think, 'is there more?'

The answer is yes.

Let's contrast each potential way of Christian living. What can we learn from each separate viewpoint?

An Old Testament focused lifestyle, as found in the pre-Gospel writings

- The God relationship is mostly focused on a patriarchal authoritarian God or Father.
- Obedience is paramount.
- The precepts and laws of God require adherence.
- The personal emphasis is on conscientious self-discipline and getting it right.
- Following the rules and doing everything according to the letter of the law is vital.
- Sacrifice, whether self-sacrifice or offerings, is the norm.
- The focus is on doing; and doing it correctly or facing punishment and/or consequences.
- Looking, waiting, searching for the promised Kingdom.

Does this ring any bells? Trying so hard to get it right and do the right thing? Fear of punishment when we fail? A God who demands obedience? Trying to be perfect?

A New Testament (Pre-Pentecost) focused lifestyle, as revealed in the Gospel writings

- The God relationship is mostly focused on the person of Jesus.
- The Cross is emphasised more than the resurrection.
- Having been mentored by Jesus, the disciples listen, learn, and practice. We don't see His followers transformed, Pre-Pentecost. They learn through trial and error.
- The personal emphasis is on learning and on **trying** to follow Jesus' teaching.
- We have divine opportunities but we are only human.
- Trying hard to understand and do the right thing while watching Jesus was the disciples' style, and ours.
- Serving and service becomes the focus, as opposed to the sacrifice we see in the Old Testament style of life.

Again, the focus is on effort, trying hard and attempting to model whatever Jesus modelled.

The New Testament (post-Pentecost) lifestyle – as revealed in post-Gospel writings

- The God relationship is focused on the transforming Presence through the Holy Spirit.
- It isn't about discipline and doing it right (Old Testament), or self-effort and doing one's best (pre-resurrection Gospels). The emphasis is on a new self, heart and spirit with a mind that is being transformed. Founded on 'It is done', it is a new, transforming life through the Holy Spirit.
- The journey does not emphasize 'doing' or following; it emphasizes becoming or being.

- The place of perfect surrender is being able to say 'I am who I am', not 'I am what I do.' Our journey is one of surrender that leads to transformation into the likeness of Jesus for His Glory.
- In the Old Testament, we see a Kingdom coming. In the New Testament (Gospels) we have the Kingdom with us in the person of Jesus. In the post-resurrection, post-Pentecost New Testament, we have the Kingdom *through* us.
- We are not waiting *for* the promised land, but are fully engaged *in* the promised land through the Kingdom within, evidenced by the outflow, the Spirit's fruit and supernatural works.

The Holy Spirit does in us what Jesus achieved for us. Surrender is one of our best opportunities for change and transformation. His inflow becomes our outflow.

The Old Testament emphasised the individual's character, role, and what they did. In the New Testament (Gospels) reformed people are doing their best to get everything right. With the coming of the Spirit in the New Testament after Pentecost, we see a transformed and transforming people.

Let's look at Peter and his journey through these three ways of being or living. Was he a good Jew prior to encountering Jesus? Doing the right thing? Offering sacrifice? Obeying the rules? Likely so. (Old Testament in orientation.)

After meeting Jesus, Peter is passionate, willing and focused on following His Master. He messes up occasionally and gets it right often; but, prior to Jesus' death, Peter was still very much Peter. He tries hard and gets some things wrong and others right. (Sound familiar?)

Peter was an enthusiast. He served hard. But it wasn't enough to win the day (the way of life before the coming of the Holy Spirit).

After the coming and infilling of the Spirit, we see a Peter who was more than the pre-resurrection Peter. Witnessing to 3000 people in Acts 5:15, a super apostle, healing the sick and moving in the power of the Spirit. People lay their sick friends relatives and neighbours on the street so Peter's shadow might heal them as he passes by. Anointing! Power! A surrendered life. A new creation and transformed man.

We need the Old Testament, the Gospels and the post gospel writings. Jesus made this clear when He said in Matthew:

> *"'Do not think that I have come to abolish the Law or the Prophets; I have not come to abolish them but to fulfil them. For truly I tell you, until Heaven and earth disappear, not the smallest letter, not the least stroke of a pen, will by any means disappear from the Law until everything is accomplished. Therefore, anyone who sets aside one of the least of these commands and teaches others accordingly will be called least in the kingdom of Heaven, but whoever practices and teaches these commands will be called great in the kingdom of Heaven. For I tell you that unless your righteousness surpasses that of the Pharisees and the teachers of the law, you will certainly not enter the kingdom of Heaven."' Matthew 5:17 - 20*

How can this be? How does Jesus fulfil the Law? He meets every standard in His perfection. In His Being, and therefore, through His doing. However, doing flows from Being. As a man thinks, so is he[2]. As a man is, so does he.

How will our righteousness surpass that of the Pharisees? In some ways, the Pharisees did not set a high standard with their religiosity and unlove. But let's suppose they set the bar high through their obsessive knowledge of the Law.

---

[2] Proverbs 23:7

We sometimes see a similar journey with new converts. Becoming a Christian might resemble the process of learning to drive a car. Initially, we realise the road requires discipline towards different rules. We try hard to concentrate, get things right, be meticulous, observe other drivers and the rules of the road. If you've driven before, you must give up bad habits to pass the test. Then, intense concentration transforms into unconscious competence; we get into the flow and driving becomes second nature.

In literal terms, we become a Christian, try to be good and please God. We look for ways and keep trying to serve and love others. Many of us are still in the Pre-Pentecost lifestyle where Christianity looks more like a self-help journey.

We try *so hard* to obey the rules, follow diligently and not fall too often. Aware of our failings and shortcomings, we try harder to overcome imperfection. After all, we are only human. We can all relate to this.

I hear the phrase 'I am only human' so often. Except that we are not. We are 'divinity in progress', (small 'd') because of Jesus. We cannot be divine apart from Him, but we can have a different life when we live in relationship with the Holy Spirit.

When did we lose our power?

We cannot have a New Testament without the Old, and the Old is the foundation for the New. We need service *and* sacrifice; surrender and service. Sacrifice, service and surrender sit together and interconnect, just like Father, Son and Spirit.

To ignore the Old Testament is neither possible, nor desirable. After all, it was the foundation for Jesus knowing His own identity. Other than communication with the Father and testimony surrounding His birth, the Old Testament was all Jesus had, from which to learn His identity. To ignore the Gospels or minimise the person of Jesus would be dangerous and ignorant. Likewise, to ignore the role and place of the Holy Spirit and His significance to our times, is to design, build and drive a car without considering fuel, direction and purpose.

Why is the power lacking? How did we lose touch with the Spirit of Jesus? Just like the Trinity revolves in a divine dance, each honouring the other, equal but different in function; so we can relate to each of them as Lord and God without bias or dishonour. The Lord, after all, is One. (Deuteronomy 6:4)

We must get to know the Holy Spirit

Few people appear to talk to have relationship with the Holy Spirit, or talk with Him. That may be because many simply don't know if it's legal to speak to Him. Most of us are comfortable speaking with Father and Jesus. When it comes to addressing the Holy Spirit, we tend to go through the Father or the Son, and say, '*Your* Holy Spirit.'

This is curious. We own the Father and speak to Him as our Father. We own and are familiar with speaking to Jesus directly. He is 'my Jesus', and 'My Father.' But when it comes to the Spirit, we seem to hesitate to build an engaging, intimate and knowing relationship with Him.

It's easy to identify who actually has relationship with Him. Listen to the people who pray in reference to the Holy Spirit and they are likely to say, 'Father, send **your** Holy Spirit.'

Perhaps this is the result of Jesus' teaching about the Holy Spirit in the Gospels. We are, after all, taught by Jesus to pray 'to the Father' who rewards what we do in secret, etc. The Lord's prayer is a prompt to pray to 'our Father in Heaven.' Surely, we only pray to Father?

Do we even have the right to speak to the Holy Spirit without demeaning or somehow disrespecting the Father or Jesus? We must resolve these questions before we find relationship with the Holy Spirit.

May I ask a question? When you pray to 'The Lord', to Whom are you praying?

We know and unequivocally accept that Jesus is Lord. It was routine for the disciples to call Him, 'Lord.'

> *'Therefore, I want you to know that no one who is speaking by the Spirit of God says, "Jesus be cursed," and no one can say, "Jesus is Lord," except by the Holy Spirit.' 1 Corinthians 12:3*

Jesus describes the Father as Lord, too. Revelation 11:15 mentions 'the Kingdom of our Lord and of His Christ'. We know that the Christ is the Son of the Father.

> *'Jesus prayed, "I thank You, Father, Lord of Heaven and earth"' Matthew 11:25*

Holy Spirit is also our Lord, as clarified in the beautiful Scripture found in 2 Corinthians 3.

> *'Now the Lord is the Spirit, and where the Spirit of the Lord is, there is freedom. And we all, who with unveiled faces contemplate the Lord's glory, are being transformed into his image with ever-increasing glory, which comes from the Lord, who is the Spirit.' 2 Corinthians 3:16-17*

As we embrace the Spirit and focus on our resurrection life – the indwelling Holy Spirit providing our purpose and our power – does the Cross become obsolete?

Did the Cross make the Law obsolete? No! The Cross was the completion of the Law, through Jesus Christ's ultimate sacrifice, selfless act of pure love, and atonement for our sin. His innocence traded for our guilt. The Cross is the pivotal place in history where Jesus cried 'It is done!'

'It is done!' was the completion of all things; the battle, struggle, and our reason for being.

As a believer, we can return to the Cross again and again in order to find freedom.

'We must move from penitence into power.' *Word of Wisdom*

I recently heard that Martin Luther spent hours in penitence, testing the limits of the priests in their confessional boxes, because he could never rid himself from the weight of guilt and the feeling of not being good enough. He spent hours confessing but never found freedom. Then he had the revelation of grace; that nothing he did could free him from the burden of sin or the tarnish from imperfection. Jesus had already won a new position for him.

Luther didn't stay at the foot of the Cross. He couldn't; he had to emerge from the mouth of the resurrection cave in order to find his future. This didn't mean he never returned to the foot of the Cross when he needed to; his life just became focused on living beyond it.

Could this be the same for you? Do you find yourself stuck in the same cycles, day after day, month after month, year after year? A new identity awaits you, friend, if you choose to find and inhabit it.

> *'For those God foreknew he also predestined to be conformed to the image of his Son, that he might be the firstborn among many brothers and sisters. 'And*

> *those he predestined, he also called; those he called,*
> *he also justified; those he justified, he also glorified.'*
> *Romans 8:29-30*

We are foreknown, called, justified, and glorified. So many times, I have heard it said that the one thing the Lord will never share is His glory, but time and again Scripture proves that He has even shared His glory with us.

'His Presence in us is also the Glory of God.' *Word of Wisdom*

He glorified us by sharing everything with us, partnering with us through the Spirit and promising us greater things. We are co-heirs and partners in Christ.

The difference between Pre-Pentecost and post-Pentecost Christianity can be clearly seen in two consecutive chapters from the book of Romans.

Life in Romans Chapter 7 or 8?

Something fundamental seems to be missing from the average Christian's life today. Most of us simply aren't living from the position of power we inherited through Jesus' death and resurrection. Just as we get to choose which tree we eat from (the tree of life or the tree of the knowledge of good and evil), we need to be aware of whether we live from Romans 7 or Romans 8; two vastly different chapters. We can easily be trapped in Roman 7 living.

So, which parts of me have not died and how do I gain victory over the flesh?

Paul works through this problem (and solution) methodically and brilliantly in the first half of the Book of Romans:

> Romans 1: Our fall
> Romans 2: Heart transformation comes from the Spirit, not from obeying the law
> Romans 3: A righteousness from God is revealed

Romans 4: Righteousness comes through faith
Romans 5: Jesus is our righteousness
Romans 6: You are set free from sin
Romans 7: Sin living in us still has power
Romans 8: We can be free from sin and death because of the Holy Spirit in us

In Romans, we see a helplessness that we cannot escape in our natural selves. Sin is at work in us, says Paul. An inherent selfishness that permeates our decisions and actions is at the core of our flesh.

> *'I do not understand what I do. For what I want to do I do not do, but what I hate I do. And if I do what I do not want to do, I agree that the law is good. As it is, it is no longer I myself who do it, but it is sin living in me. For I know that good itself does not dwell in me, that is, in my sinful nature. For I have the desire to do what is good, but I cannot carry it out.' Romans 7:15-18*

No amount of well-meaning, trying hard, willpower, self-effort, enthusiasm, counselling or planning will free us from the inherent sinful nature. We return again and again, like a dog to its vomit (Proverbs 26:11) to our addictions, selfishness, greed, sin, and weakness.

> *'For I do not do the good I want to do, but the evil I do not want to do—this I keep on doing.' Romans 7:19*

So, from where does our rescue come? Paul tells us that our rescue comes through Jesus. Look at the rescue in Chapter 8:1-2, where,

'THE LAW OF THE SPIRIT OF LIFE HAS SET YOU FREE FROM THE LAW OF SIN AND DEATH.'

We know and understand the Law of Sin and Death; but what is the Law of the Spirit of life? Let's dissect Romans Chapter 8 in order to find out.

The Law of the Spirit provides us with:

Romans 8:1	Freedom from condemnation
Romans 8:2	Freedom from sin
Romans 8:2	Freedom from death
Romans 8:4	Righteousness in the sight of the Law
Romans 8:6	A mind filled with life and peace
Romans 8:8	A life pleasing to God
Romans 8:10	An alive spirit
Romans 8:11	Life in our mortal body
Romans 8:12	Ability to put misdeeds of the body to death
Romans 8: 14	Identity as a son of God
Romans 8:15	Relationship with 'papa God' or Abba.
Romans 8:17	Co-heirs of God status
Romans 8:17	Co-heirs with Christ status
Romans 8:29	Predestined conformity to the likeness of Jesus
Romans 8:30	Standing called, justified, glorified
Romans 8:35	Standing never separated from God's love
Romans 8:37	The position of more than conquerors
Romans 8:39	Standing inseparable from God's love

All this, because of Jesus and the Spirit. But we must choose to participate in the Law of the Spirit of life as opposed to the old covenant law of sin and death.

In Romans 8, we are given the choice to:

Romans 8:4	Live according to the Spirit
Romans 8:5	Have our mind set on what the Spirit desires
Romans 8:9	Be controlled by the Spirit
Romans 8:13	By the Spirit, put to death the misdeeds of the body
Romans 8:14	Be led by the Spirit
Romans 8:17	Become Co-heirs with Christ if we share in Jesus' suffering

Powerful. Let's develop a relationship with the Spirit of God. We can because of Jesus. We can because of the Father.

Heart, Mind and Spirit

The Old Testament and the Law could only achieve a limited framework for life in relationship with God the Creator. The Law provided a framework for a life consecrated to God. The consciousness of God prevailed through ritual and rules; since the Jewish Nation lived by rituals, dates, weekly and annual feasts and celebrations.

Their God-consciousness resulted from a life punctuated by behavioural reminders: dates and times and rituals. What the Law could never do was win heart, mind and spirit. We could use this illustration: The Law is to the Christian what a skeleton is to a human being – a framework. Although the skeleton isn't the heart, flesh or organs, we can't omit the skeleton from the body. The body could not stand, otherwise.

The post-resurrection new covenant relationship, following Jesus' death and the Holy Spirit's release on all mankind, is the living flesh on the law; the heart, mind, and breath.

> *'The law is only a shadow of the good things that are coming—not the realities themselves. For this reason, it can never, by the same sacrifices repeated endlessly year after year, make perfect those who draw near to worship.' Hebrews 10:1*

Through the Holy Spirit, we have the transformation of mind, heart and spirit. We have rebirth. Remember Nicodemus, the Jewish Priest, who (too embarrassed by day) visits Jesus at night to ask questions? Jesus tells him that he must be born again.

> *'"How can someone be born when they are old?" Nicodemus asked. "Surely they cannot enter a second time into their mother's womb to be born!" Jesus answered, "Very truly I tell you, no one can enter the kingdom of God unless they are born of water and the Spirit. Flesh gives birth to flesh, but the Spirit gives birth*

> *to spirit. You should not be surprised at my saying, 'You must be born again.' The wind blows wherever it pleases. You hear its sound, but you cannot tell where it comes from or where it is going. So, it is with everyone born of the Spirit.'" John 3:4-8*

The command here is to be born of water (water baptism) and the Spirit (Spirit baptism). To enter the Kingdom of God we must have died His death (water baptism) and we must have experienced resurrection from death (infilling of the Spirit). Sadly, we have learned to compartmentalise. The reality of life is often far more tangible than that of the Kingdom from which we inhabit this planet: Heaven. We are seated in the Heavenly realms with Christ Jesus (Ephesians 2:6).

Let's discover how we become lovers of the Father, partakers in His Presence, Co-heirs and partners with Jesus as Lord. It's not too late.

> *'Therefore, do not let anyone judge you by what you eat or drink, or with regard to a religious festival, a New Moon celebration or a Sabbath day. These are a shadow of the things that were to come; the reality, however, is found in Christ.' Colossians 2:16-17*

Just as the prophet in South Africa challenged me, may I challenge you with a question?

How Deep Is Your Fellowship with The Holy Spirit?

It is easy to identify those with a relationship with the Spirit. Many people pray and talk about the Spirit in a way that suggests that they do not have an intimate connection with Him. It's so easy to pray, 'Father, send your Spirit', but what made the Spirit belong to the Father and not to you?

Is Jesus your Jesus? Do you talk with Him freely? Look for Him in the Word? Talk with Him in order to build relationship? Are you learning to love, obey, hear, and know Him? Or is Jesus 'the Father's Jesus? Do you go through the Father in order to relate to Jesus?

Is the God the Father your Father? Or do you speak to Him through Jesus – 'Can you tell your Dad...?' The Holy Spirit is *your* Holy Spirit who longs to have a relationship with you, reveal more of the Lord to you, communicate more, and converse with you.

Of the three ways of living outlined by the Old Testament, New Testament Pre-Pentecost and New Testament after the Holy Spirit has immersed His life in ours, it is difficult to separate Pre-Pentecost and Post-Pentecost believers in terms of lifestyle. The Pre-Pentecost disciples we read about in the Gospels did everything Jesus did – they cast out demons, healed the sick, and worked miracles. They had the authority of Jesus. But they still didn't have the transformed identity we find in Post-Pentecost believers.

The future was decidedly precarious for Pre-Pentecost Christians. For Post-Pentecost believers, the infilling and transformation of the Spirit makes the difference. Not self-effort or trying hard to overcome, but being seated in the Heavenly realms with Christ Jesus and living through the flow of God from inside out. We see a journey.

Talk with and listen to the Spirit of the Father, the Spirit of Jesus: The Holy Spirit.

CHAPTER 5 – THE TESTIMONY OF JESUS

An Emerging Story

Someone once said your life might be the only Bible others get to read. Your life is on display for the glory of God. Despite being two thousand years beyond the Pentecost experience described in Acts 2, we are still new to the life and potential of the Spirit of Jesus in and through us.

> *"Very truly I tell you, whoever believes in me will do the works I have been doing, and they will do even greater things than these, because I am going to the Father."' John 14:12*

You are not merely the only Bible others might ever read, i.e., the encounter with Jesus people need; your life is also an extension of the Book of Acts. *Acts continues the supernatural story of love.*

Remember 'the journey of becoming' discussed earlier in this book? As I read the Sermon on the Mount in Matthew, the revelation hit me. If we are transformed into the likeness of Jesus through His Spirit, then the Sermon on the Mount ceases to be about (often difficult and painful) choices and decisions; living ceases to be about what we do. We actually **become** the Sermon on the Mount through inner transformation by the Spirit. The life of Jesus *in* us, becomes the life of Jesus *through* us.

> **'Fruit doesn't work hard to grow on the tree.'** *Word of Wisdom*

We have so much more to unlearn than to learn.

One hope is identified in Romans 12:1-2: the renewing of our minds brings transformation. Is it possible that we have forgotten to seek God? Have we become 'teaching' as opposed to 'Presence' centric? In our gatherings, has teaching on how to behave somehow become our highlight instead of the revelation of His Presence?

God is a God of speech. He has so much to say. Just look at the Bible. But are we listening? You see, the world is so busy. We might say life is busy, but I make a distinction between 'the world' and 'life.' If Jesus said 'I am the life' then we cannot compromise our concept of life with our experience of the world. Life in Jesus must be perfect and full, if He is the life. We are on a journey of finding this life in all its fullness.

> **'Apologetics are what we have left when we live without power.'** *Word of Wisdom*

Are we prepared to be wrong? The most frightening Christians are those who believe that their theology is correct at the expense of other Christians who, by default, are 'incorrect.' And if we are honest, don't we all secretly believe our own view of the Bible is the correct theology?

Looking Like Love

I was handing out sweets and roses on the streets one Saturday with several people from 'church'. We were 'on mission.' Scott called me over. He is a gifted evangelist who would run from being called an evangelist.

'Karen, I'm having an interesting conversation with that guy.' He said, 'Can you come over and help?'

I'm always ready to support the team if they need it; to look like love on every occasion.

I was meeting Matt. Tall, dressed in black, with a demonic image on his T Shirt, about 25 years old. He looked like a gothic with heavy black eye shadow, dark eyes, studs in his ears and a nose piercing – an inverted hook pointing outwards. John was expressionless.

Starting a conversation is always difficult. I tend to start conversations at first base, establishing if there is a belief in God in order to open up dialogue.

'Do you have a spirituality, Matt?'

He looked faintly awkward. 'Yes, I do.' He paused. 'I work for the other side.'

Curious. Who was the 'other side'?

'I work for Satan,' he said calmly.

We had a starting point! (The goal is to always look like love, not to win battles.)

I asked him about his life – how he ended up working for the other side, what brought him here today and why he was talking with us. Surely a divine appointment.

Matt said he grew up in a Christian family and went to church in his early years. 'Something happened' at church, and he left Christianity and decided to work for Satan. My heart went out to Matt and his Christian family. They were probably praying for an encounter just like this for their prodigal son.

'You are the encounter many people are praying for.' *Word of Wisdom*

Give Love A-Way

Matt said, among other things, that the devil had promised him freedom. I reassured him of Jesus' love for him. I spoke about the history of the devil – cast out of Heaven and defeated through Jesus and the Cross. Acting on love and speaking in the Spirit, I told Matt to call upon the Name of Jesus if (or when) he ever discovered Satan was lying to him about freedom, or needed help. Matt needed to know that no name can withstand the most powerful Name in the universe, and that Jesus had not turned away from him. On the contrary, Jesus is always just one call away.

'Can we pray for you?' I asked.

The power in these encounters comes mostly from what God does when we pray with the person.

Surprisingly, Matt said yes. He had listened, expressionless but calmly throughout.

How to pray? Could we lay hands on him if he is filled with the enemy? Could there be a negative transmission of his demonic power if we did? The thought was fleeting; however, my faith in the blood of Jesus was stronger than any fear of demonic attack. Our faith allowed us to lay hands on Matt and pray.

His body trembled as we prayed, and I was filled with love for this brave, young one who had turned so harshly away from the God he knew, to mistakenly yet wilfully obey a liar, thief, murderer and destroyer. The thief had lied to him about freedom.

That was our encounter. A step in Matt's journey. A seed sown, waiting for the Harvester to harvest. Setting him up for his next encounter with Jesus.

How easy it is to shake our heads at Matt for turning from God and tell him how wrong he was to believe a lie. To say he faced eternal damnation in hell for worshipping Satan. Instead, I did what I know best. Look like love and pray. Accusation didn't bring me to Jesus. His Love found me.

Scott and I prayed together after this encounter. We prayed for Matt, his future and family. We 'prayer washed' in the blood of Jesus, freed ourselves from any curses past, present or future, and carried on with our work. What a day!

> **'Compassion is the flow of love in our brokenness; the decision to love without judgement.'** *Word of Wisdom*

In Romans 1:16, Paul says he is not ashamed of the gospel – God's power bringing salvation for all who believe. In its purest sense, the gospel fulfils the two greatest commandments – to love God with heart, mind, soul and strength; and love your neighbour as yourself. The gospel is not a gospel of judgement, but of love. We share the gospel not to judge, condemn or force our view onto others, but because God is Love (1 John 4:8). He loves to love.

The fruit of the Spirit in us is love, joy, peace, patience, goodness, faithfulness, gentleness and self-control. Self-control is our ability to make a Heavenly choice.

> **'Self-control is the tap through which the other fruit of the Spirit flow.'** *Word of Wisdom*

Love is the currency of Heaven. Jesus said our role is not to judge but to love. We can't beat the unsaved into submission in the name of the law. We move people toward the Kingdom in the name of love.

Engagement with the Holy Spirit frequently attracts controversy — the flesh at war with the Spirit; the letter of the law attempting to stifle the way of the Spirit. In Romans 8, Paul says the law of the Spirit of life frees us from the law of sin and death.

> **'Signs and wonders are our greatest opportunity for communicating the gospel.'** *Word of Wisdom*

The Holy Spirit moved through the post-Pentecost disciples in a way we did not experience in the Gospels. They broke new ground and performed miraculous signs and wonders. What is a wonder? Anything that makes you wonder!

Where a church is inhibited by its building and walls, and hopes to attract rather than extract, persuasion and argument can become the primary vocal tools for sharing the gospel. Apologetics becomes the tool of the day. Yet nothing speaks more loudly or convincingly of God than a miracle, sign or wonder.

Two notable passages:

> 'The apostles performed many signs and wonders among the people. And all the believers used to meet together in Solomon's Colonnade. No one else dared join them, even though they were highly regarded by the people. Nevertheless, more and more men and women believed in the Lord and were added to their number. As a result, people brought the sick into the streets and laid them on beds and mats so that at least Peter's shadow might fall on some of them as he passed by. Crowds gathered also from the towns around Jerusalem, bringing their sick and those tormented by impure spirits, and all of them were healed.' Acts 5:12–16

It's no coincidence that with signs and wonders come increase in the church. It's so easy to regain our power; stepping out and praying for folk creates opportunities for more miracles, signs and wonders. I remember hearing a believer bemoan the fact that God no longer does miracles, and asking me why. We, His hands, feet and heart on this planet, are the conduit for His Spirit, preparing the way for His return.

'We are full of miracles if we are full of the Spirit.' *Word of Wisdom*

In the Book of Acts, the believers were so feared, held in awe, and powerfull that nobody dared join them. Bring on that day! There were huge expectations as people brought their sick onto the streets to be healed by Peter's shadow! Astounding. An emerging gospel. Just as we see an emerging journey through the Bible, this emergence continues today.

The NHS is bursting at the seams with patients, yet we are the only legitimate and safe people to administer supernatural healing. Why are there queues? Why aren't we going? What are we equipped to do that we aren't?

A religious audience might cry out 'sacrilegious!' Many Christians often slate men and women of God in communion with the Holy Spirit due, I believe, to the threat they pose to the enemy's kingdom. Attacks are focused on those who step out in faith and see powerful works of the Holy Spirit in their ministries. Whole swathes of the Christian community appear to be more focused on defending the Christian faith than expanding the Kingdom through love. Can't God take care of His own church? Reliance on the Presence of God to solve most, if not all issues is our best weapon and line of attack.

Everyone was healed, Luke says in the Book of Acts. Everyone. Don't we want that? Don't we long for the day when Cancer is no longer dignified with a capital C, and believers become cancer killers as opposed to cancer doing the killing? Is this just a pipedream? Or is it a possibility because of His indwelling Spirit? It is a challenge. Like having a destination but no road map. The roadmap is the Word of God and the destination is Jesus. We must press into the Word and our search for the Lord.

What God ever asked to be sought? Yet, numerous verses invite us to 'seek Him'.

> *"'Ask and it will be given to you; seek and you will find; knock and the door will be opened to you. For everyone who asks receives; the one who seeks finds; and to the one who knocks, the door will be opened.'" Matthew 7:7-8*

The second notable passage is this:

> 'God did extraordinary miracles through Paul, so that even handkerchiefs and aprons that had touched him were taken to the sick, and their illnesses were cured and the evil spirits left them.' Acts 19:11-12

This happened while Paul was in Ephesus. Ephesus was steeped in occultic and temple worship of gods and goddesses (like Artemis), daily ceremonies, festivals and celebrations. It was a hard place to be a Christian, yet Paul thrived in this environment.

The Holy Spirit's life in believers created a wave of faith and expectation that led to supernatural occurrences every day. Why aren't the greater things Jesus spoke about happening now? Because we aren't stepping out and doing them. Only the Holy Spirit can transform us. He turned a bunch of working-class guys into the most extraordinary people on the planet.

That is our potential.

Surrender Isn't Weakness

The world teaches that surrender looks like weakness – a white flag held above the trench. But to the Christian, surrender is strength. It is empty hands held out, ready to be filled. Offering the old for the new. The low path where self becomes less important and we consider others first. When we give God our all, ready to be led and trusting Him with the outcomes. We give Him all we are and have.

We stop struggling. Surrender.

We stop fighting. Surrender.

We allow Him to go ahead while we stay in the moment.

The enemy has been clever on two counts. Buddhists focus on the death of ego or self, and miss out on the Cross; the only place for redemption. New Agers believe in their own divinity, missing out on the One who is the Way, the Truth, and the Life. Religion is ultimately empty without the Spirit of God inhabiting its core. Through His death on the Cross, Jesus created a bridge to the Father, and through His purity, a way for us to be pure, too. With no yesterday and no tomorrow. Just the fullness of today, within, through His Spirit.

Conclusion

Our understanding of God and His possibilities is emerging. The more we seek, the more we find. Our relationship with the Holy Spirit is an emerging journey of discovery as we go deeper into God and search for His fullness. Our search for and discovery of God is an emerging journey, which is why we are called to seek Him. Our identity and place in Him is an emerging journey, as we are transformed by Him from 'glory into glory.'

Embrace the Holy Spirit. Be ready to listen to His instruction. He is ready to speak with you.

> *'But the anointing that you received from him abides in you, and you have no need that anyone should teach you. But as his anointing teaches you about everything, and is true, and is no lie—just as it has taught you, abide in him.' 1 John 2:27 (ESV)*

We have to find our reality in the life of the Holy Spirit today. He is the only one who, despite our circumstances, can revive, enliven, inspire and direct us to live differently, abundantly and victoriously.

Talk with and listen to the Spirit of the Father, the Spirit of Jesus: The Holy Spirit.

CHAPTER 6 – THE TWO TREE KINGDOM

Grow Fruit from the Tree of Life

In order to love well, we must be sure about the tree we eat from and the fruit we bear.

When we look closely at the two trees found in the garden of Eden, we find a powerful relevance for us today. Let's examine them.

> *'Now the Lord God had planted a garden in the east, in Eden; and there he put the man he had formed. The Lord God made all kinds of trees grow out of the ground—trees that were pleasing to the eye and good for food. In the middle of the garden were the tree of life and the tree of the knowledge of good and evil.'*
> *Genesis 2:8-9*

There are many trees in the garden, all pleasing to the eye and good for food. Mankind had only one command from God at that time:

> *'And the Lord God commanded the man, "You are free to eat from any tree in the garden; but you must not eat from the tree of the knowledge of good and evil, for when you eat from it you will certainly die."' Genesis 2:16-17*

Just one command to obey. It's interesting that fruit from the tree of life was available to be eaten, but not fruit from the tree of the knowledge of good and evil.

The fruit from the latter brought self-consciousness, or consciousness of self, causing the barrier between us and God. Eating from this tree brought shame, fear, death; every negative compulsion known to man. It became the gateway for sin and judgement. We suffer from its effects even today. Yet this tree probably looked like every other tree in the garden. Pleasing to the eye. Attractive. Alluring. But it was forbidden fruit.

To disobey God is to put self above God.

'Sin is our selfishness prioritised.'
Word of Wisdom

At this point, the way to the tree of life is withheld from Adam and Eve, and they are banished from the garden of Eden. God makes clear that to eat from the tree of life is to attain eternal life, or the ability to live forever.

What a terrible concoction for mankind, to have eaten first from the tree leading to pain, suffering and ultimately death, with the possibility of its destructive consequences continuing into eternity. Thank God for Jesus, our tree of life. We can eat from His fruit and find freedom from sin and inherit eternal life. Just beautiful. How humbling, that the third most significant tree on the planet, a planet created by Him and for Him, is found in the form of the Cross.

Misled into eating from the tree of the knowledge of good and evil, Eve and Adam were deceived into believing a lie, with mankind's future eternally altered by one self-centred decision. Would we have been so foolish as to succumb to that temptation today with the benefit of hindsight? Many of us still eat fruit from the same tree as Eve and Adam. We have the same choice and reap the same consequences.

Let's imagine the fruit on the **tree of life** as the fruit of the Spirit – nine types of fruit, all pleasing to the eye:

*'But the fruit of the Spirit is **love, joy,***
peace, forbearance, kindness, goodness,

> ***faithfulness, gentleness*** *and **self-control**. Against such*
> *things there is no law.' Galatians 5:22-23*

The fruit on the tree of the knowledge of good and evil is equally alluring, but different in outcome. Thinking is polarised and we now have judgement and the moral stance. One thing is good. Another is evil. Someone is right, another wrong. Judgement, mostly focused on people who are not us, has become a part of our psyche, which, I believe, is why Jesus taught us not to judge. We are 'displeased' with other people's behaviour, lifestyle, actions. Displeased, even, with who the other person is.

If we aren't discerning, we will chew on this fruit every day. We look at others and make judgements on their lives and actions. We have a very definite opinion about how they have got it wrong or right.

> 'He shouldn't do that.'
> 'If only she did this, it might look like that…'
> 'You're not right.'
> 'You're wrong.'

We can't help judging others unless we surrender to Jesus.

'But what if our judgements are correct?' I hear you cry.

That's okay, if you are the designated judge. To my understanding, the only safe judge is our Heavenly Judge, Jesus.

> *'For as the Father has life in himself, so he has granted the Son*
> *also to have life in himself. And he has given him authority to*
> *judge because he is the Son of Man.' John 5:26-27*

Too often, we confuse discernment and judgement, and change our attitude towards our neighbour as a consequence. We even eat this fruit in relation ourselves. Every broken thought about yourself comes from eating fruit from the wrong tree.

'I'm bad.'
'I don't deserve love.'
'I can never get things right.'
'I'm not worthy.'

If we walk in this fruit, our outreach to others may be Old Testament-focused. We could get to murderous extremes in polarising good and bad where the 'bad' becomes our enemy and an obstacle to survival. Judgement then becomes our weapon for protection and change.

> 'Instead, speaking the truth in love, we will grow to become in every respect the mature body of him who is the head, that is, Christ. From him the whole body, joined and held together by every supporting ligament, grows and builds itself up in love, as each part does its work.' Ephesians 4:15-16

If the fruit hanging from you were visible, metaphorically speaking, would they be prickly pears or the fruit of the Spirit?

Getting back to Matt, the young man working for 'the other side'; that wasn't a 'them and us' situation. I didn't speak from the tree of the knowledge of good and evil and say 'what you're doing is wrong and offensive to God.' I told the truth.

'Perhaps the freedom Satan promised you won't materialise,' I said. 'Jesus will be there for you, ready when you call.' No name is more powerful than Jesus Christ, the Son of God.

God is so capable of finding and meeting people who don't know Him. We are there to help, witness and testify to the truth, power and love of Jesus; not judge our neighbour who might well be lost. There's nothing like experiencing judgement and the pain of rejection to motivate us to look like love in all circumstances.

'Love draws people in; judgement pushes people out.' *Word of Wisdom*

I find the term non-Christian unhelpful. It implies a situation with me in the 'in' group and the others outside of it. I prefer the term 'Pre-Christian'. It implies a journey towards Jesus and doesn't exclude others from having their own journey. This doesn't mean everyone eventually embraces Jesus; it means everyone has the opportunity.

Love is an invitation along that journey towards the Greatest Love the world has ever known. Jesus. If you set your heart to build up and not tear others down, God can take care of the rest.

'Revelation, and not explanation, provides insight.'
Word of Wisdom

How attractive is a Christianity led by love? It's my personal opinion that it is impossible to teach anyone anything. But that doesn't mean that others can't learn from us. We are sowers. We sow the seed and the Farmer (God) harvests the crop. That doesn't mean God can't or won't work through hard-hitting messages confronting people with the need for a choice.

The type of outreach I'm describing here is accessible for everyone, rather than the gifted few. Loving your neighbour.

A man in my church has a senior role in the City of London. Most lunchtimes, you will find him handing out tracts, preaching on street corners and exhorting people to come to Christ. He is faithful, loving and committed, and I have the utmost respect for him. He scatters the seed daily, and in proportion to the seed he faithfully sows, he occasionally witnesses a positive outcome. Others then reap where my friend in London has sown. When I go to the streets to out-reach, I also harvest where others have sown.

> *"Don't you have a saying, 'It's still four months until harvest'? I tell you, open your eyes and look at the fields! They are ripe for harvest. Even now the one who reaps draws a wage and harvests a crop for eternal life, so that the sower and the reaper may be glad together. Thus, the saying 'One sows and another*

> *reaps' is true. I sent you to reap what you have not worked for. Others have done the hard work, and you have reaped the benefits of their labour."* John 4:35-38

Once again, we come back to the question: 'what is outreach?' A smile? A door held open? It is choosing to look like love. Refusing to condemn. Refusing to judge. Demonstrating love. Loving can be hard work. It's always a choice and when we love, we scatter seeds.

Time and again, when I have asked God for words or pictures for people looking for a spiritual connection, His words are positive, powerful and meaningful. To be honest; they can be shocking. Where I would like to keep a record of wrongs, prompt people not to fall short of His standards, or point out that there's another way; the words from God are usually affirming, loving and lifesaving.

He is so hard to relate to, yet so good, endlessly loving, kind and affirming. I don't understand God sometimes, to be honest.

Choose to Look Through the Lens of Love

'But I can see the error of their ways!' You might cry. Pointing out errors in others only creates barriers, division or alienation.

Focus on the best in that person; focus on their potential in Heaven. We know Jesus died for everyone but not everyone has appropriated the gift of salvation. Every person on the street, on this planet, has technically been saved by the Cross. But not everyone knows it.

> *'My dear children, I write this to you so that you will not sin. But if anybody does sin, we have an advocate with the Father—Jesus Christ, the Righteous One. He is the atoning sacrifice for our sins, and not only for ours but also for the sins of the whole world.'* 1 John 2:1-2

Let's not get into a theological battle here. Don't put me into a theological box and label me as unsafe. I'm not saying everyone is saved (I could be wrong). What I *am* saying is that Jesus died for everyone, and everyone deserves to know about this gift; the gift of life through Jesus. It's why I do what I do when I outreach.

How did we become so expert in judging others, especially Christians whose theology differs from our own? They are wrong and I am right by default. It's the tree of the knowledge of good and evil.

Are you prepared to be wrong?

Let's make sure we are seeing others through the lens of love, and not one of judgement. Love is a hand extended. Judgement is a hand withheld.

We see Jesus looking like love. Not asking how the person got into their mess, but offering healing, compassion, deliverance. We can, with His Spirit in us, choose the same path.

Talk with and listen to the Spirit of the Father, the Spirit of Jesus: The Holy Spirit.

CHAPTER 7 – RECOGNISING THE OPPORTUNITY

Whose is Your Life?

> *'For our citizenship is in Heaven, from which also we eagerly wait for a Saviour, the Lord Jesus Christ;'*
> Philippians 3:20

At the beginning of Mission School with Heidi Baker in South Africa, each staff member of staff had to introduce themselves by name and place of origin. Jackie stood up, and with a broad Scottish accent, declared, 'My name is Jackie, and I come from Heaven'. This was met with much laughter from the 250-plus students, but Jackie didn't resubmit her place of origin.

Was this just an amusing anecdote? I recall thinking in amusement at the time, 'I must remember that joke and use it myself'. But actually, where you believe you are from, and where you belong now, influences everything you do and think. It will inform you and others about who you are.

And so, may I ask you to consider which Kingdom you inhabit?

Give Love A-Way

A friend and I booked to have coffee in Colchester Town centre. Not unusual. We talked and laughed, and made our way in to Town. God had taught me not to pray in its formal sense i.e. on my knees for lengthy periods, (this was my journey and may not be yours), and not to *do* but to *become* evangelism. Ever since, I have walked with my head in Heaven. What does that mean? I walk with an awareness that I don't belong to this planet. I belong to Heaven. Everything I see and hear has the lens of Heaven covering it. You might call it always being God-conscious. Which is what He did to me when He showed me that my Christian life was compartmentalised into segments (prayer, outreach etc), and not a continual walk or flow in the Spirit.

I am performance-oriented. My life broken into a series of daily habits, tasks and procedures. But God simply 'is', and can teach, train and transform us into 'being', too. Look at the beautiful Book of Ephesians to find out where you are placed:

> *'And God raised us up with Christ and seated us with him in the Heavenly realms in Christ Jesus, in order that in the coming ages he might show the incomparable riches of his grace, expressed in his kindness to us in Christ Jesus.' Ephesians 2:6-7*

Anyhow, back to coffee with my friend in Colchester. We talked and walked, and because my head is in Heaven, I walked with the awareness of God, open and alert for the God-opportunity. If it happens, I'm ready. If it doesn't, it doesn't. Most of the time, when someone steps into my space and engages with me, I usually believe, naively, that God sent them to me. If a conversation ensues, it's likely to be a divine opportunity or appointment. If a conversation doesn't happen, nothing is lost.

My friend and I were almost at the Coffee House when a young guy selling a subscription to a charity stepped up and introduced himself. My friend looked irritated. He was a street seller. He wanted money.

I was alert to the moment because he stepped into my space. He began with some flattery and tried his sales pitch, which was fine. It's how he makes a living. But I love to go deep with people. Perhaps it's the psychologist in me. Why waste time on a superficial conversation that doesn't deal with the meaning of life when you could have a real divine encounter?

So, I asked him my standard question for going deeper, further.

'Do you have a dream in life? Something you'd love to be or achieve?'

What this question says to the person is: 'I'm interested in you and I care about your response. I am invested and rooting for you to be the best you can possibly be. There's more to life than you see, and you matter.' It is choosing to look like love. How many people enter our world each day that we simply ignore?

> *'"They are not of the world, even as I am not of the world."' John 17:16*

Treat everyone like they matter

The young guy and I got into a conversation. I probably asked him if he believed in God, at some point. I know the conversation went well, in that, he engaged, I engaged, and he allowed me to pray for him on the street. Meanwhile, my friend was getting impatient.

We walked on from there to the café and I offered to buy the coffee. As I waited in the queue, I glanced at one of the baristas. The eyes are 'the window to the soul'. A quick look can tell us so much. A quick glimpse at the barista's face because I cared, and in that moment, I 'knew' in the Spirit that she was having a difficult time. God downloaded a deep sense of where this young woman was at, and some of why she was in this place. Then it was my turn in the queue, and the young woman turned to serve me. Now, I could let this go or deliver a message of love from Jesus. I decided to gently impart some words from the Lord to her, recognising that she was working and might find this difficult.

When I give a word to a person I don't know or meet 'by chance', I generally say, 'I know this is weird, and you probably won't meet me again. I love Jesus, and He sometimes gives me a message for a person I meet. When I saw you, I felt him tell me something about your situation. May I share it with you?'

If they respond with 'yes', I share. If 'no', I respect that.

Many times, the prospective recipient will look slightly anxious, as though a message from God is a rebuke from a nasty headmaster.

In which case, I say, 'It won't be anything horrible. Just words to encourage you in your journey at this time.'

I delivered a message about Jesus helping with her finances, recognising that this was a tough time for her. That He knows, loves, and is with her.

Tears poured down her face. 'But how do you know these things?' She asked. 'It's so true.'

'I don't know them, but Jesus does.' I replied. 'He showed me.'

That was the sum total of the encounter. It was sowing a seed for another to harvest on another day. Pointing to and glorifying Jesus, the Giver of Love.

By this time, my friend was staring at me, frustrated as I carried the coffee to her and sat down at the table.

'So sorry,' I said. 'I needed to deliver a message to the coffee barista.'

My friend scowled. After a while, she said, 'It's not fair. You get all the opportunities to outreach and I don't get any.'

My friend had felt hassled by a young guy selling a charity subscription and walked past the barista because she had come in for coffee and not for Kingdom.

We belong to a different Kingdom

We can be so invested in (distracted by) the world, our feelings, beliefs, and lives, that we miss the opportunities around us to witness and testify about the Kingdom we come from.

> *"If the world hates you, you know that it has hated Me before it hated you. "If you were of the world, the world would love its own; but because you are not of the world, but I chose you out of the world, because of this the world hates you." John 15:18-19*

I pray for healing because it's one of the commandments Jesus gave us, and not because I enjoy it.

One day, I was sitting with a Christian friend in a church café when one of his clients came in unexpectedly to see him about his accounts. The client didn't look well.

'Are you okay?' I asked. 'You don't look well.'

He wearily took a seat. 'I haven't been well for some time. The doctors aren't sure what it is, but I've had it for some months now.'

My heart went out to him. How would I feel if I had felt unwell for months and no one knew why?

'May I pray for you?' I asked. 'I don't know if you have a faith, but I know Jesus can make a difference.'

My Christian accountant friend looked horrified. It was one of those 'oh no' moments many Christians seem to dread. Indeed, I dread it, too, when praying for healing. I've prayed for many folks who haven't experienced healing, and many folks who have.

The client said I could. I took this as faith and prayed my best prayer. Mark Marx from Healing on the Streets teaching says to simply pray your best prayer when you pray for healing.

I left my friend with his client and moved on. Around three weeks later, I heard that the client had felt much better afterwards, and was now completely healed. Just great. Sowing a seed. Looking like love.

How many times do people tell you in one week that something is awry with their health, family, finance, or life? How easy is it to say, 'Would it be ok to pray for you? It won't take two minutes.' Then pray. Because there is power in Presence. And when you pray, the Presence of God is always there.

Delivery drivers, the postman, in the supermarket, walking down the street, walking the dog, the children, in the bus, wherever you are, you are the solution to the world's greatest problems. You might be the divine encounter a person has been waiting for; that someone else has prayed for. Don't we all want our loved ones to be witnessed to in an authentic and powerful way?

Who enters your space?

> 'For our citizenship is in Heaven, from which also we eagerly wait for a Saviour, the Lord Jesus Christ;'
> Philippians 3:20

Yes, you might appear weird. You probably are, because you don't belong to this planet. Jesus said so. The Bible said it.

> 'All these died in faith, without receiving the promises, but having seen them and having welcomed them from a distance, and having confessed that they were strangers and exiles on the earth. For those who say such things make it clear that they are seeking a country of their own. And indeed if they had been thinking of that country from which they went out, they would have had opportunity to return.' Hebrews 11:13-16

Give Love A-Way

I have a beautiful friend called Flora who is in her 70s, but looks like she is 40. She walks around 20 miles per week, and definitely isn't from this planet. Flora has drawn a metaphorical circle around her, and whenever someone steps into that metre surrounding her, she considers this an invitation to look like love, skip the superficial, and engage in a Heaven-focused conversation. Flora's one line conversation opener is, 'Do you worship around here?'

'Karen, it's brilliant!' Flora tells me. 'Most people have no idea what I'm talking about, and so I have to tell them.'

Flora doesn't switch off, even when sales people ring on her phone. They have entered her space. And God has probably sent them. When someone rings her, canvassing or cold calling, Flora doesn't treat them like a nuisance. Her focus is on the Kingdom, and not this planet.

Who knows, but the way we treat others is the way we are treating Jesus, He tells us. The telephone sales person has entered her sphere, her space, and she treats each person like a divine appointment.

Flora says, 'I can give you five minutes.' She listens, and then says, 'Now that I've given you five minutes, can you give *me* five minutes of *your* time?'

With that, she tells them about the goodness of Jesus, and has led several people to Jesus over the telephone.

May I challenge us? If we treat anyone as inconvenient or unplanned (including cold-callers), or like an irritant, we might unknowingly miss our opportunity to be love on a planet dying from selfish irritation.

Didn't Jesus say, 'whatever you did for the least of these, you did for me?'

> "Then the righteous will answer him, 'Lord, when did we see you hungry and feed you, or thirsty and give you something to drink? When did we see you a stranger and invite you in, or needing clothes and clothe you? When did we see you sick or in prison and go to visit you?' "The King will reply, 'Truly I tell you, whatever you did for one of the least of these brothers and sisters of mine, you did for me.'
> Matthew 25:37-40

We are walking witnesses. Our lives are being read day by day, moment by moment. We cannot forget who we are, why we are here, or our purpose on this planet.

The Kingdom has other subjects who don't yet realise that they have royal parentage, an inheritance and an incredible, eternal future ahead of them.

Go to the supermarket, yes, because you need groceries, but also to engage with anyone stepping in to your space. Greet the cashier on the till with a 'how is your day going?' 'Your smile makes a difference, thank you.' Find something to compliment; a reason to smile.

Have you ever travelled abroad? The customs, laws, and language may be different. *We* feel like we are different; like a stranger in a foreign place – slightly or even significantly out of place.

As citizens of Heaven, what seems normal to this world is not normal for us. We may look the same on the outside, but everything is different inside. We have a new mind and heart given to us by God. We don't think or feel the same. Our goals and desires are likely to be different.

Christianity was never an appendage to our life, an insurance policy to keep us safe from anxiety or fear when trouble comes, or even an enhancement to our experience in this world. It is death to the self who lived by the world's standards, and separation for Heaven. We have so much to unlearn.

> *'And he died for all, that those who live should no longer live for themselves but for him who died for them and was raised again.' 2 Corinthians 5:15*

What is our purpose on this planet?

> *'Do you not know that your bodies are temples of the Holy Spirit, who is in you, whom you have received from God? You are not your own; you were bought at a price. Therefore honour God with your bodies.' 1 Corinthians 6:19-20*

If we are travelling through this planet to get to our promised land where there is no death, pain or tears, it is feasible to think that our time here has a purpose. Where and when we were born, our personality, looks, and heart are all meant for such a time as this. We have been lent to this planet for a purpose. If we focus on hedonistic pleasure or even survival, we miss out on so much. We put up with broken identity and lack of fire for too long.

The world teaches us to focus on career and accumulate wealth. Then we might buy bigger homes and better cars. After our paid working life is over, we can retire, take it easy and become more hedonistic in our outlook because we have earned it.

There is nothing wrong with wealth, if that's what God has provided us with. Money itself is not the root of all evil, as you know, but the love of money breeds selfishness. How we use it and whose we consider it to be are Kingdom issues.

Does your wealth belong to you or God? Are you a steward or treasurer? It's so easy to be complacent with accumulated things (wealth, belongings, possessions, families).

I sold my first house 15 years after I first bought it for 4 times its purchase value. The mortgage was cleared.

'I've done quite well'. I thought idly, one day.

Soon afterwards, I read about another person who thought exactly the same in the Book of Daniel: Nebuchadnezzar.

> Twelve months later, as the king was walking on the roof of the royal palace of Babylon, he said, "Is not this the great Babylon I have built as the royal residence, by my mighty power and for the glory of my majesty?"
> Daniel 4:29-30

Nebuchadnezzar is immediately humbled, leaves the royal palace and lives like an ox, eating grass. Are our lives truly surrendered to God? Are we stewarding resources for the kingdom or for ourselves? Are we attentive to how God might want to use us and our resources? Have you asked Him?

There is so much to fulness of life that we haven't even begun to encounter. Most of the time, I feel that God follows me and my plans, and not the other way around.

Who is leading us?

Are we attentive to Him when we shop? Are our eyes and thoughts fixed on Jesus? What would the world look like if they were? What if the realities of this life—our jobs, homes, friendships, and social lives—were given over to the cause of the Kingdom? What if we listened attentively to the voice of Heaven?

Is our present relationship with the Holy Spirit mirrored in the Israelites' relationship with God, as seen in the Book of Exodus? It appears the majority were largely removed from God and fearful. They didn't have the intimacy God had with Moses. Let's take a closer look at Moses and his intimacy with God.

Talk with and listen to the Spirit of the Father, the Spirit of Jesus: The Holy Spirit.

CHAPTER 8 - DESENSITISATION AND DISCONNECT

How to Heal

Is there a cure to desensitisation and disconnection from God? The answer is YES. Many of our lives have become largely both desensitised to God and disconnected from Him. We are ingrained with values shaped by the media, stereotypes, our upbringing, history and present—all largely informed by the world, mostly learned and taught from an early age. We often spend more time caught up in electronic media than the Word of God. We have so much more to unlearn, than to actually learn.

When we look at the life of Moses, though, we can take heart. Moses was probably one of the most messed up guys in history. Look at the evidence.

Born into a time of genocide, with uncompromising Egyptian slave drivers demanding impossible work quotas through violence and force (and we think we have it bad?), the Israelites have no value other than as slaves and forced labour to the Egyptians. For almost 400 years, the Israelite's God appears to have abandoned His chosen ones.

Moses' parents are interesting.

> *'Amram married his father's sister Jochebed, who bore him Aaron and Moses. Amram lived 137 years.' Exodus 6:20*

Moses' parents are Levites, his mother is also his grandfather's sister. So interesting that, when God later details the laws around sexual relations to Moses in Leviticus, He states:

> *"'Do not have sexual relations with your father's sister; she is your father's close relative.'" Leviticus 18:12*

We can only wonder at the dynamics within the family on hearing this. Even knowing this commandment, Moses had to focus solely on obedience to God. The messages we deliver are a challenge at times.

Moses is one of three children: Miriam, the eldest, Aaron, and, three years later, Moses is born.

A psychoanalyst would need hours to get to grips with Moses and his psyche. His mother is forced to hide her good-looking new-born son. The other two children are kept at home, but Moses is technically abandoned. In effect, she abandons him to fate, God, or both, by placing him in the Nile in a basket. From here, it gets complicated as Miriam runs along the bank, spots Pharaoh's daughter and her servants pulling Moses out of the water, and suggests,

'Shall I get one of the Hebrew women to nurse the baby for you?'[3]

Here we get to the beginning of secrets in Moses life. Miriam fetches her own mother and Pharaoh's daughter pays her to bring up the child until he is old enough to live with her in the palace. From poverty to prince? Moses' mother is unlikely to confess at this stage that Moses is her own child. We know later on that Moses has a strong sense of his people and identity, because when he grows up, he watches 'his own people', the Israelites, at their hard labour.

---

[3] Exodus 2:7

Moses' name, which he is given when Pharaoh's daughter adopts him, sounds like the Hebrew for 'draw out.' The very root of his pain, shame and displacement is the name by which he becomes known. He can never escape his past with a name like Moses.

He is given away as a young boy by his mother and Israelite family to live in the foreign environment of Pharaoh's court. How did he look? Was he treated with the privilege and honour equal to an Egyptian son? Was this Israelite slave child now a prince? Could he discuss his own family with his new Egyptian adopters, or did he have to remain silent in order to protect their identity (father, mother, sister, brother) from Pharaoh's daughter and the court? A completely new culture, new gods, new customs. Was he equally despised by the Israelites and Egyptians? How could he know his true identity?

Anger, like a coiled spring inside him, waits to be released. He is so messed up that he murders in an Egyptian in cold blood, hastily buries the body, and doesn't expect to be discovered. He is betrayed by one of his own people; an Israelite who witnesses the murder. Then he is betrayed by his own people; his grandfather Pharaoh, hears of this and tries to kill Moses. Chaos in the court.

Moses is seriously messed up. On what should be one of the happiest occasions of his life, he names the son—born to him by his new wife—Gershom, meaning: 'I have become an alien in a foreign land'.

If your life has been messy and you feel disconnected from society and the world in general, take heart! Your life is ripe for intimacy with God. If you have suffered rejection and life's trajectory always slopes downwards, take heart! Your life is ripe for intimacy with God.

Moses' identity was so messed up, he didn't know who he was. How could he? Could God really use a man like this to change the course of history? Can God really use a person like you to change the course of history? Of course, He can.

Moses' emotions were repressed and driven down by difficulty. As a shepherd to his father-in-law, he drives the flock to isolated places, probably licking his wounds and biding time until time passes. When he sees a burning bush, he is merely curious because his emotions are desensitised. The first thing God does in this encounter is to 'ground' Moses.

> "Do not come any closer," God said. "Take off your sandals, for the place where you are standing is holy ground." Exodus 3:5

So, Moses stands on the soil in his bare feet. God is certainly the first and greatest psychologist to exist! So often, a person damaged by society will struggle to relate to, trust or even identify with people. What God says to Moses must be music to his ears. 'Don't come any closer.' How wonderful.

This God knows us so well, He even understands our psyche and what we need most. But He doesn't leave us in that same place. He restores us. Mends us. Heals us. Holds us.

Existing or living?

When we exist, when everything feels the same and life is an endless grey path, we can lose sight of the technicolour Kingdom, and the riches and splendour of our Creator God.

> **'Labels from anyone other than God are most likely counterfeit.'** *Word of Wisdom*

How did Moses' brokenness manifest? In a broken identity. Look at the five limiting beliefs he uses to persuade God not to commission him for His purpose on this planet. Each limiting belief is rooted in a different fear.

'Who am I?' (Exodus 3:11) Moses' self-esteem is so low that he doesn't feel worthy of God's call. The fear attacking him is *doubt*. The solution to doubt is God's promise to always be with you. Your equipping is **God with you**.

The second limiting belief is his challenge that he doesn't know God well enough to complete the task. In effect, he says, **'I'm not ready yet.'** Exodus 3:13. The fear attacking him here is *anxiety*. Anxiety is a disease that tries to rob us of the right view of God. The fear is that God isn't powerful enough to sustain Moses in his calling. The solution? God reveals His name: **'I am who I am.'** What more is there to know other than that I AM has called you?

The third excuse Moses uses is, **'But what if?'** 'What if?' can stop us in our tracks. The disease here is *worry*; imagining possibilities that become the obstacle to actually saying yes to God. FEAR—False Expectations Appearing Real—can trap us into never moving forward, never progressing. It comes disguised in a whole host of plausible excuses chaining us into position. The fear is the unexpected. And what solution does God offer to Moses? **'...and these signs shall accompany you.'** Exodus 4:8. The same promise Jesus gives us.

> "And these signs will accompany those who believe: In my name they will drive out demons; they will speak in new tongues; they will pick up snakes with their hands; and when they drink deadly poison, it will not hurt them at all; they will place their hands on sick people, and they will get well." Mark 16:17 - 18

Supernatural signs and wonders are given to soften hearts (like Pharaoh's) and challenge unbelief, allowing God to testify on His own behalf. If you never see signs and wonders, step out more and pray for more Pre-Christians.

The fourth excuse Moses gives to God is to tell him **'I'm not equipped to serve you.'** Exodus 4:10. If we believe that we aren't equipped then we are believing a lie, because our equipping comes from Him.

Recently, as I was fretting about resources and lifting my need to God, the revelation hit me that my fear about lack of resource or provision was not the main issue, even though it had become the main focus. The main issue was a *lack of trust* in God as my Provider (Jehovah Jireh). All I need is found in Him. David says in Psalm 23: 'The Lord is my Shepherd; I shall not be in want.'

The Lord is the resource. He is the equipping. The disease here is that Moses' beliefs about himself limit his capacity to serve God. When we believe this, we are somehow saying God isn't enough; that His capacity in us won't meet our need. In Exodus 4:13, God promises to help and to teach Moses. Isn't that exactly what God has promised us through the Holy Spirit; a Counsellor and Teacher? The enough you need is the Holy Spirit. The more that you need is **The Spirit of God**.

Finally, Moses' fifth reason for provoking God not to use Him in His purposes: **'But others are better than me.'** Have you ever said that?

'You've got it wrong, God. Others could do a far better job.'

For some of us, this is ingrained into our psyche. We have to surrender and allow God to transform the broken part. The sickness in this case (sickness because it erodes from us the fullness of our walk with Jesus) is *pride*. We are actually telling God, 'I think you have it wrong. I know better than you.' How easy it is to fall in to this trap. When the next big invite comes from the church, you might feel someone else is better equipped for the job. Ultimately, this is pride. That, in saying He trusts and wants to use us, God isn't telling the truth. His view of me doesn't match my view of who I am or what I can achieve. The solution here, is to **get to know God better**.

You aren't alone.

Give Love A-Way

God identifies Aaron, his older brother, to accompany Moses which, at face value, looks like a blessing. But this is the brother the family kept when Moses was abandoned; the brother complicit in Moses' suffering. Thankfully, God persists with Moses in all his brokenness and utilises his personality and past to achieve the greatest of outcomes for Israel.

Thank God that He persists with us in our brokenness, through all our excuses. We don't want to miss our potential. Your life has purpose, and in the same way He used Moses, God can use you. Not with the same task or mission, but with a task suited to you and your gifts.

From being a broken man at the beginning of Exodus, we see Moses, in chapter 33, in an intimate and close relationship with the same God he earlier hid his face from:

> *'Now Moses used to take a tent and pitch it outside the camp some distance away, calling it the "tent of meeting." Anyone inquiring of the Lord would go to the tent of meeting outside the camp. And whenever Moses went out to the tent, all the people rose and stood at the entrances to their tents, watching Moses until he entered the tent. As Moses went into the tent, the pillar of cloud would come down and stay at the entrance, while the Lord spoke with Moses. Whenever the people saw the pillar of cloud standing at the entrance to the tent, they all stood and worshiped, each at the entrance to their tent. The Lord would speak to Moses face to face, as one speaks to a friend. Then Moses would return to the camp, but his young aide Joshua son of Nun did not leave the tent.' Exodus 33:7-11*

Imagine speaking to God face to face. Such was the Presence around Moses that, as he walked to this tent of meeting, people rose and stood to observe the Lord appear in a cloud to speak with Him face to face, like a friend.

From fear to intimacy

How did this happen? Through time, trust, listening, sitting in the Presence and engaging with God. Through honesty, trial, messing up yet again (in another display of temper, Moses smashes the two tablets imprinted with the Ten Commandments, written by the finger of God).

Look at Moses' next conversation with God, which possibly summarises the core message of this whole book:

> *Moses said to the* Lord, *"You have been telling me, 'Lead these people,' but you have not let me know whom you will send with me. You have said, 'I know you by name and you have found favour with me.' If you are pleased with me, teach me your ways so I may know you and continue to find favour with you. Remember that this nation is your people." The* Lord *replied, "My Presence will go with you, and I will give you rest." Then Moses said to him, "If your Presence does not go with us, do not send us up from here. How will anyone know that you are pleased with me and with your people unless you go with us? What else will distinguish me and your people from all the other people on the face of the earth?" Exodus 33:12-16*

Moses is known by name, and has found favour with God, just like you. He knows you by name. But here is the power: Moses can now enter that place of rest; the place from which everything else flows. The 'still' place, with God.

The Lord tells Moses His Presence will go with him; from which comes rest. How hard we sometimes work to find the Presence when actually, the Presence—His Spirit—is in, on and around us, and will never leave us, just like Jesus said.

'He doesn't need our hard work. He needs our surrender.' *Word of Wisdom*

But here is the key to identity and purpose: Moses says there's no point in going if the Presence of the Lord doesn't go with them.

Effectively, Moses says, 'What else will distinguish me and your people from all the other people on the face of the earth?'

The Presence of God. We may have good works, achievements, big plans, high ideals, or strategy for growth, but what differentiates us from the rest of the world is His Strong Presence.

Do you believe that about yourself? That His Presence in you is power? You have the power of God inside you, around you and on you!

> *"But you will receive power when the Holy Spirit comes on you; and you will be my witnesses in Jerusalem, and in all Judea and Samaria, and to the ends of the earth."*
> Acts 1:8

Miracles were never primarily meant for the church. We have to get out of our buildings.

'His transforming power in us changes the ordinary into extraordinary.' *Word of Wisdom*

Peter simply walked along a street, and people brought out their sick to catch his shadow. The Presence of God.

'We are limited only by our understanding of His possibilities in and through us.' *Word of Wisdom*

My friend Barbara and I went searching for encounters in our local town. We sat on a bench, but no one stepped into our space. As a rule, I smile and talk to passers-by about, well, anything really—the weather, time of day, etc. If they engage with me, it is a sign that meeting them may have a purpose. It doesn't always work, but sometimes it's enough.

It was grey and overcast on this particular day. There was a wide expanse of path ahead. As we sat chatting together, we didn't notice a man walking towards us. I saw him just as he went to pass by, smiled and said 'Hello'.

His life mattered. I want everyone to know their life matters. Saying hello makes this easy to convey. He said hello, then stopped in his tracks, mid-stride, rooted to the pavement.

Barbara and I looked at him. He looked at us. He didn't move. I stared at him, expecting him to speak. He didn't.

'Are you okay?' I asked.

'Yes,' he replied. 'But I can't move?' Said almost like a question.

Barbara and I exchanged puzzled looks. The man seemed confused and slightly afraid.

'You're welcome to pass by.' I offered.

'But I can't,' He said after a few seconds, sounding distinctly uncomfortable. 'I have to get to the dentist, but I can't move. Why is this happening?' The man was literally stuck in position. It was one of the most amazing wonders I had ever encountered.

I explained who we were, why we had come to town, and said I felt God had probably held him in position. It was the start of a great conversation, and five minutes later, he was off to the dentist as planned!

Seeds.

His Presence is all we have to differentiate ourselves from the ordinary. This is why the Holy Spirit is so important to us. Moses met with God through a cloud descending to the location of their meeting. God has met with us through His Spirit in exactly the same way. Except, the Ark of the Presence isn't a box or an object. YOU are the host carrying His Presence. In essence, you are the human ark!

If you engage with the Holy Spirit—if you live with the awareness that the WHO inside you will change your home, neighbourhood, city, and nation—your life will never be the same.

How far does His presence in you extend?

> **'Belief in what is possible leads to the fulfilment of the impossible.'** Word of Wisdom

If you go into a shop and believe His Presence in you can touch everyone in that shop, it will certainly happen. You may not see the result. Then again you may.

If you believe your every step creates a consecrated area for the Lord, it will be so. His memory remembers far more than ours. You may forget where you have walked, but God certainly won't.

Two of the most powerful words Jesus ever spoke were these:

> 'While Jesus was still speaking, some people came from the house of Jairus, the synagogue leader. "Your daughter is dead," they said. "Why bother the teacher anymore?" Overhearing what they said, Jesus told him, "Don't be afraid; **just believe**."' Mark 5:35-36

'Just believe' or 'only believe' makes everything possible. Jesus didn't say, 'work really hard to prove yourself' or 'try hard to be a good Christian'. He simply said, 'Just believe.'

In biological terms, the Holy Spirit filling us is the closest we get to experiencing intimacy with God. The Holy Spirit in us is the consummation of the love relationship with God.

> **'The Holy Spirit in you is the intimacy with God you are searching for.'** *Word of Wisdom*

To abide in the Spirit is the place of rest. We see this in Jesus' pivotal teaching on the Spirit found in chapters 14, 15 and 16 of John's gospel.

Rest doesn't mean inactivity. Rest just means that He becomes the outflow from you, from His inflow in to you.

Bill Johnson, a leader in Bethel Church, Redding in the United States, holds up a new and unopened bottle of water during the conference at which he is speaking.

'How do you know if this bottle is full?' He asks. After a few brave suggestions from the onlookers, he opens the bottle and squeezes it, so that water spills out. 'Because it is overflowing.' He says.

> **'To rest in God is to fully allow His Lordship in our lives.'** *Word of Wisdom*

What transforms Moses from murderer into hero? From a man who isolates himself by herding his flock away from society, to a national leader? From a man out of touch with his feelings and driven to impulsive acts by rage to a national leader and friend of God? No doubt psychiatrists today could label Moses with a Personality Disorder, Sociopath, any host of labels. But Moses is God's man.

The one label we must heed is the one God places on us: Son, Daughter, Beloved.

'Labels won't stick unless we choose to wear them.' *Word of Wisdom*

What transformed Moses? Time spent in the Presence of God. Moses finds the place of rest—often found through trial and trusting.

Look at this beautiful Scripture before the parting of the Red Sea. This is the place of ultimate defeat and despair. Led out from Egypt by Moses, the Israelites find themselves with no way forward (the Red Sea ahead) and no way back (penned in by Pharaoh and the entire Egyptian army). Immense pressure is on Moses. The Israelites don't appeal to God; they prefer to complain to their leader. (Ever been in that place? Are you in it now?)

Moses steps out in faith. He releases the word of faith in tremendous adversity, although he cannot know what God has planned. He promises the Israelites that they will see the deliverance of the Lord TODAY! Prophetic vision and resolute faith.

This one Scripture is ideal to learn both at the heart and head levels:

> *'"The Lord will fight for you; you need only to be still."' Exodus 14:14*

A place of rest. We all know the victory achieved that day.

'Time in the Presence of God will bring transformation.' *Word of Wisdom*

Moses' father-in-law, Jethro helped Moses obtain the place of rest, too. He sees Moses at work, acting as judge and arbiter for the Israelite nation from morning till evening (Exodus 18). Moses is acting exactly like a poorly socialised person—independently. He hasn't considered teaching and delegation, structure or team. It is when Jethro advises him that Moses truly becomes a leader; choosing 'capable men' from all over Israel to oversee thousands, hundreds, fifties and tens, and to adjudicate in legal disputes.

Moses had been working too hard, when his calling was simple: to stay in the Presence and listen to God.

Being in the Presence of God is like a person who lies on a sunbed to obtain a sun tan. They cannot know the changes happening as they lie under ultraviolet rays, but when they come out from the bed, the effects are visible and obvious – tanned skin. After time in the Presence, Moses' face shines so brightly, he has to cover His face.

You won't necessarily see or even feel the effects, but others will.

May I encourage you to Son-bathe?

Talk with and listen to the Spirit of the Father, the Spirit of Jesus: The Holy Spirit.

CHAPTER 9 – JESUS' VIEWS ON THE HOLY SPIRIT

Discovering the Fullness of God

Do we really think it's okay to talk to the Holy Spirit? We still know so little about Him. One of the most profound statements I have ever heard from a charismatic teacher is that we treat the Holy Spirit like an After Eight mint at the end of a meal: not essential, but nice to have. Life could be so exciting if we let the Holy Spirit be Lord.

Can we even speak with Him? Is it heresy to imagine we can? What does Jesus teach about the Holy Spirit?

Tertullian, a third century lawyer, originated the concept of the Trinity. In the book of John, we clearly see the full beauty of what we now understand as the Trinity; or a triune God, with three distinct parts. We see this incredible relationship where Father honours Son, Son honours Father, Father and Son honour the Holy Spirit, and the Spirit honours the Father and the Son. Perfect unity.

In the beginning we see God creating the heavens and the earth. The name commonly used for God in the Old Testament is the Hebrew word *Elohim*, which is plural in form. It is also found in the singular form of *El* and *Elah*, used individually to describe Father, Son and Spirit in different Scriptures. We see the plurality of God emerging from His very name.

Holy Spirit was there at the beginning of creation; hovering over the waters, creating something from nothing. The Holy Spirit cannot have more honour than to be placed in the first chapter and verses of Genesis. He was prominent in the beginning.

The imagery of the Spirit hovering over nothing influences how I pray. I bring my emptiness, my nothingness, and wait in silence to allow the Holy Spirit to create something out of the nothing I bring.

'An empty me in exchange for His fullness.'
Word of Wisdom

The Hebrew for Spirit of God in Genesis 1 is *Ruach Elohim*, a feminine noun, meaning breath, wind or spirit. The very breath of this trinitarian God forms creation from nothing. This is relevant because we might otherwise find a confusion of God identities, roles and promises in John.

> *"And if I go and prepare a place for you, I will come back and take you to be with me that you also may be where I am." John 14:3*

Did you ever wonder how Jesus would fulfil that promise to His disciples? He just told them that He is going away, and that He will come back so they might also be where he is. How is that possible? Do we have evidence of that, other than His appearing to His disciples for 40 days after His resurrection? The possibility comes to us through the Holy Spirit, or through the Spirit of Jesus as He is known in several Scriptures (Romans 8:9, 1 Peter 1:11, Romans 8:8), including:

> *'Because you are sons, God has sent forth the Spirit of His Son into our hearts, crying, "Abba! Father!"' Galatians 4:6*

This is enormously significant. You actually have the Spirit of Jesus within you. The Jesus you are seeking is within you. He couldn't be in one place physically, as He was with His disciples in the Gospels. The world would be too big for him to lead as one man, and so He came back, by His Spirit, to take us safely back to Himself. Jesus says:

> *'On my account you will be brought before governors and kings as witnesses to them and to the Gentiles. But when they arrest you, do not worry about what to say or how to say it. At that time, you will be given what to say, for it will not be you speaking, but the Spirit of your Father speaking through you.'* Matthew 10:18-20

The Spirit is also the Spirit of the Father! Speaking through us.

Two plural nouns are applied to God. God and Lord are almost always plural when applied to God. The nouns God (*Elohim*) and Lord (*Adonai*) are the two most frequently used to describe God in the Old Testament. The concept of the 'three persons in one' God can be a source of contention. Jehovah's witnesses don't recognise the Divinity of Jesus; Mormons don't believe the Holy Spirit has the same substance as the Father and the Son, believing that the Holy Spirit has no physical form. We sometimes find these same beliefs in mainstream Christians who, perhaps, are unaware of who the Holy Spirit really is.

In fact, Holy Spirit takes many forms, not least, I believe, the human form as suggested by the creation of man.

> *'So, God created mankind in his own image, in the image of God he created them; male and female he created them.'* Genesis 1: 27

'To miss out on the true identity of the Spirit is to miss out on the full identity of God.'
Word of Wisdom

Most weeks, a small team and I go into Colchester to talk to people about Jesus whenever the opportunity arises. My friend Flora was once in conversation with a guy in his 20s. He was on crutches. The conversation was happening beside the table of another Christian church denomination who don't believe the gifts of the Spirit are in operation today, but finished 2000 years ago.

I don't remember what came first, the young guy giving his life to Jesus, or being healed. We prayed for the pain in his foot to go, and for full movement in his leg. For some reason, I then left Flora with the young man. Five minutes later, an excited Flora called me over.

'Karen, LOOK!'

The young man was walking away, holding his crutches in the air, almost skipping and certainly laughing. Completely healed! I glanced over at the man holding his tracts, and wondered what he thought, as everything had happened beside him. There was no reaction at all. He simply looked on.

How much we miss when we choose not to fellowship with the Spirit of God. What a waste of a friendship.

Why did Jesus emphasise to His disciples that they should pray to the Father? Is it wrong for us to speak to the Spirit? If the Lordship of God has three parts—with an indivisibility among the three—can it be wrong to communicate with the Spirit of God?

Jesus arrived after the Old Testament times, during which God was known by a variety of names but rarely called Father. He was called the Father of the Israelite nation twice (Deuteronomy 32:6, Isaiah 63:16), and the Father of certain individuals fifteen times.

"Father" was Jesus' favourite term for addressing God—some 65 times in the Synoptic Gospels and over 100 times in John. It would have seemed revolutionary, perhaps even heretical, that Jesus called God Father, or even Abba, a more intimate term. This personalising of God enraged the religious people. We are immediately birthed into sonship and a personal relationship with God when we identify Him as Father. And Jesus directs His disciples to pray to God as Father, too, in the Lord's prayer. 'Our Father, who art in Heaven.'

Jesus says what we do in secret will be rewarded by the Father, and that we should pray to the Father who is unseen. Jesus steadfastly pointed to the Father.

When Steven is stoned in the Book of Acts, he cries out to Jesus. Paul talks about calling on the Name of the Lord Jesus Christ (1 Corinthians 1:1–2). And of course, Jesus commanded us to pray in His Name. I believe that we haven't fully understood the meaning of praying in Jesus Name, because HIS Name is so vast, so hallowed, so big, that it is impossible to grasp the fullness of its meaning and application.

Praying 'in the Name of Jesus' is not like a prayer insurance policy that guarantees a response. It's more like a position to inhabit, guaranteeing authority.

So, we come back again to the Lordship of God. Father as Lord. Jesus as Lord. The Spirit as Lord.

In this evolving Gospel, we make sense of the Spirit's role, and whether or not we are able to talk with Him, by examining John 14, 15 and 16. Once again, a religious perspective might blind us from engaging in this relationship, so, understanding what Jesus reveals to us about the Holy Spirit's nature and role is vital.

Jesus mediates between our spiritual past and future. He transformed our backward-looking view of God as Father, as exemplified in the Old Testament, to a completely new perspective. Jehovah became Dad. Likewise, Jesus shifts our forward-looking view of God as Spirit, as exemplified in the New Testament. Holy Spirit becomes our colleague, teacher, guide.

We must catch up with a new move of God, pointing us toward the sovereignty and importance of the Holy Spirit in our everyday lives. The Holy Spirit is exciting! He brings life!

For how long can we continue with a Christianity that can look more like a social movement than a spiritual revolution?

Why are young people turning to alcohol for kicks? Alcoholic drunkenness is a counterfeit for Holy Spirit fullness. Why are so many people self-medicating to survive? Is it because we have offered them a rule book instead of love? Or are Pre-Christians kept away by the brick walls of our buildings?

Our aspiration and hope can only be a Holy Spirit-led inspiring, empowering, enlivened church, in touch with God and connecting people to the Father, Jesus and Spirit.

We must fellowship with the Spirit as Paul directs us:

> *'May the grace of the Lord Jesus Christ, and the love of God, and the fellowship of the Holy Spirit be with you all.' 2 Corinthians 13:14*

'We misunderstand prayer if we believe we cannot pray to the Holy Spirit. Prayer is not just about petition, but more about relationship. The very *Ruach* of love.' *Word of Wisdom*

Thomas, bless him, wants to know where Jesus is going. Jesus says He is the way, the truth, the life[4]. Of course, no one can come to the Father except through Jesus. He is the exact representation of the Father! To know the Father is to know Jesus, because He is in the Father.

We must try not to use the Bible as a barrier with people we believe aren't like us. We sometimes wave this Scripture sagely as though we know who will favourably encounter God and who won't, based on their beliefs alone. To God, our heart's condition is more vital than lip service. This is a radical thought: instead of using Scriptures to brutalise and bruise (I know, because I've done it), can we leave all judgement to God and simply get on with love?

Jesus encourages us to ask HIM for anything in His Name and He will do it (John 14:13). Does this contradict His earlier teaching directing us to pray to the Father who is, as yet, unseen? Or is there an evolutionary understanding, a discovery of the fullness of God that enables us to pray to Lord as Father, Son, and Spirit? We must decide.

> *"And I will ask the Father, and he will give you another advocate to help you and be with you forever— the Spirit of truth."' John 14:16-17*

Who will 'give you another helper'? The Father.

> *'"When the Advocate comes, whom I will send to you from the Father—the Spirit of truth who goes out from the Father—he will testify about me."' John 15:26*

Jesus will send the Spirit *'from the Father'*.

---

[4] John 14:5-7

> *"But very truly I tell you, it is for your good that I am going away. Unless I go away, the Advocate will not come to you; but if I go, I will send him to you."' John 16:7*

Jesus will send the Spirit? This isn't divine confusion, but divine revelation around whom our God is; this Triune God. The name for the Spirit is truth, yet Jesus describes Himself as the way and the truth, too.

It's so interesting that the world cannot accept the Spirit, because it 'neither sees Him nor knows Him.[5]' This has a major implication. That we **can see and know** the Spirit because we accept Him. Yet many are still not accepting Him. We might receive Him in principle and yet have little to no relationship with Him.

Is the Holy Spirit God? Deuteronomy 6:4 and Mark 12:29 reference Father, Son and Spirit as God and One Lord. The Holy Spirit is God. We are baptised into the name of the Father, Son and Holy Spirit (Matthew 28:19)

> *'Peter said, "Ananias, how is it that Satan has so filled your heart that you have lied to the Holy Spirit and have kept for yourself some of the money you received for the land? Didn't it belong to you before it was sold? And after it was sold, wasn't the money at your disposal? What made you think of doing such a thing? You have not lied to men but to God."' Acts 5:3-4*

The Holy Spirit is not the subservient helper. He is the Creator Himself, found in the person of Jesus, known also as Father.

One of my spiritual heroes, Elmer Towns, says in his magnificent book; *The Names of the Holy Spirit,* that we know more about Jesus who spent thirty years on this planet than we know about the Holy Spirit who has been here for almost 2000 years. A tragedy.

---

[5] John 14:17

The Role of The Spirit is Defined by His Names

In the book of John, Jesus used the term *parakletos* to describe the Spirit four times. *Parakletos,* a Greek word, is translated helper, comforter, counsellor, advocate, or one called alongside. Jesus promised to send another Comforter or Helper.

Here the Greek word for 'other' is *allos* which means 'the same of a kind'. Jesus could have used another word, *heteros,* for other, meaning of a different kind. Jesus is identifying both Himself and the Spirit, as of the same substance i.e. Lord, or God.

The biggest mistake believers can make is to believe we are ordinary. We are not. The Holy Spirit is called alongside us to comfort, help, counsel. Isn't that something we all want and need; to have Jesus with us 24/7? The Spirit of Jesus with, in, upon, around you. To be with you for ever, just like Jesus, who says 'I will never leave you nor forsake you'[6]. He is with us through *His* Spirit.

Who was the Father to the Israelites in the Old Testament? God, helper, teacher, advocate, stand-by. Who was Jesus in the New Testament pre-resurrection? God, helper, teacher, advocate, alongside. Who is the Spirit in our post-resurrection life? God, helper, teacher, advocate, alongside. Whoever heard of a counsellor that you could not confer with? A comforter that you couldn't share with? A teacher you cannot learn from, confide in, question, hear and obtain direction from?

Talk to the Holy Spirit; He is your friend, too.

What else does the Spirit do, according to John 14-16? Jesus calls Him:

- The Counsellor or Advocate - four times (John 14:16; John 14:26; John 15:26)

---

[6] Hebrews 13:5

- The Spirit of Truth - three times (John 14:17; John 14:26; John 15:26; John 16:13)
- Jesus calls the Spirit 'He', not 'it' on every occasion
- He is holy, identified as Holy Spirit by Jesus (John 14:26)
- He will be with you forever (John 14:16)
- You will know Him (John 14:17)
- He will live with you (John 14:17)
- He will be in you (John 14:17)
- He will teach you all things (John 14:25)
- He will remind you of everything Jesus has said (John 14:26)
- He will testify about Jesus (John 15:26)
- He will come to you (John 16:7)
- He will be sent to you by the Father (John 14:26)
- He will be sent to you by Jesus (John 16:7)
- He will convict the world with regard to sin, righteousness and judgement (John 16:8)
- He will convict the world of sin because men don't believe in Jesus (John 16:9)
- He will convict the world with regard to righteousness, because Jesus is going to the Father (John 16:10)
- He will convict the world of judgement, because the prince of this world now stands condemned (John 16:11)
- He will guide you into all truth (John 16:13)
- He will tell you what is yet to come (John 16:13)
- He will bring glory to Jesus (John 16:14)
- He will take what belongs to Jesus and make it known to you (John 16:14)

One last reference to this Triune God:

> *'All that belongs to the Father is mine. That is why I said the Spirit will receive from me what he will make known to you.' John 16:15*

The evidence for the Lordship of the Spirit?

> *'But whenever a person turns to the Lord, the veil is removed. Now the Lord is the Spirit, and where the Lord's Spirit is, there is freedom. As all of us reflect the glory of the Lord with unveiled faces, we are becoming more like him with ever-increasing glory by the Lord's Spirit.' 2 Corinthians 3 16*

Around 740 BC, the Prophet Isaiah reveals the identity of 'the Lord Almighty';

> *'For to us a child is born, to us a son is given, and the government will be on his shoulders. And he will be called* **Wonderful Counsellor, Mighty God, Everlasting Father, Prince of Peace**. *Of the greatness of his government and peace there will be no end. He will reign on David's throne and over his kingdom, establishing and upholding it with justice and righteousness from that time on and forever. The zeal of the* LORD *Almighty will accomplish this.' Isaiah 9:6-7*

The Son will be called Wonderful Counsellor (the same name given to the Spirit); Mighty God (the generic name for Father, Son and Spirit). The Son is also known as Everlasting Father (the same name given to the Father). Evidence for the lordship of God: Father, Son and Spirit.

Mind blowing. When we are praying to 'the Lord' or to 'Almighty God', we are praying to the Father, Son, and Spirit. We are not precluded from talking to the Holy Spirit, who is God.

We talked about the journey of becoming and the importance of 'Being' as the new place of transformation. As 'becomers' of Jesus, tangibly and intentionally residing in Him and He in us leads to walking in His will every day.

Still on these three pivotal chapters in John—14, 15, 16—Jesus makes our position clear in Chapter 15. The Greek word translated here is *meno* which means 'abide' or 'remain' or 'stay'. Jesus commands;

- Remain in me (John 15:4 [twice]; John 15:5; John 15:7)
- I will remain in you (John 15:4; John 15:7)
- Remain in the vine (John 15:4)
- Remain in my love (John 15:9; John 15:10)
- Remain in the Father's love (John 15:10)

Ten references to abiding in ten verses! We have to know that place of rest. What indicates that we possibly haven't found that place? How many people do you know who live from a place of joy?

> *'I have told you this so that my joy may be in you and that your joy may be complete.'* John 15:11

And after this, Jesus commands us to love each other as He has loved us.

'The inflow of His love *within* us becomes the outflow of His love *through* us.' *Word of Wisdom*

Are we intentionally walking in His love as beacons of light to the world? Or do we look like the rest of the world; closed off to His voice; our will being done and not His?

Is our world a greater reality and priority than the Kingdom within us? We have so much to learn, to surrender and take in.

'The Word transforms.' *Word of Wisdom*

I believe God gave me a wonderful revelation about the fruit of the Spirit. He showed me that the fruit were listed in an order that was an intentional communication from Heaven.

The fruit of the Spirit follows a logical sequence:

> **Love** is first.
>
> If love my neighbour, I am likely to have **joy**, because I hold no judgement.
>
> If I have joy, I will inhabit a place of **peace**, because joy overrides disquiet. We cannot have disquiet and be joyful!
>
> Peace breeds **patience**. Unruffled, unsettled, and at ease.
>
> If I have patience, I will flow in acts of **kindness** because we have no barrier in our relationship.
>
> The consequence of kindness is **goodness.**
>
> In this position of goodness, no matter what happens, love remains **faithful**.
>
> In my faithfulness, I bring a **gentleness** to love.
>
> Finally, no matter the prevailing conditions in a relationship, all of this fruit combined leads to **self-control**. I can control myself, continue to look like love, be filled with joy and flow in the fruit because of my relationship with the Spirit.

These are fruit. A consequence of relationship with the Holy Spirit. They grow through abiding.

I also felt God revealing through this that few of us manifest joy because we rarely focus our purpose on love. How do we demonstrate the fruit of love? By abiding in and receiving the Father and Son's love within us. Time in the Presence.

> *'...but those who hope in the* LORD
> *will renew their strength. They will soar on wings like*
> *eagles; they will run and not grow weary,*
> *they will walk and not be faint.'* Isaiah 40:31

The Hebrew translation for the word 'hope' used above is *qavah*, meaning to 'wait'. Waiting isn't passive. It's a position of surrender and listening. We are on a journey of be-coming. A journey of transformation into the likeness of Jesus. We are 'be-coming.'

> *'And we all, who with unveiled faces contemplate the Lord's glory, are being transformed into his image with ever-increasing glory, which comes from the Lord, who is the Spirit.' 2 Corinthians 3:18*

How do we get to the place of abiding? Mystics like Brother Lawrence and Madam Guyon from centuries past focused on and achieved the place of abiding. Part of the difficulty is that we label in order to intellectualise or distance ourselves from things we are unsure of or haven't personally encountered. Labels can create observers. Listening to the Spirit becomes 'contemplative prayer' and witnessing to people becomes 'evangelism'.

Men and women of God sought to walk, conscious of God, with an intentional mindset; abiding just like Jesus called us to do.

'This is a journey.' *Word of Wisdom*

Techniques for Abiding

1. Finding this place is a personal journey. We grow through revelation, not always through explanation. It was revelation when God showed me that I think backwards (regurgitate thoughts, people and events); and pray forwards (pray for what is ahead). This stops the endless rumination, thinking and analysis we can so easily become trapped in. Live in the now.

2. Abiding will come from knowing your identity. Jesus says you are not of this world. We have a Kingdom that is our inheritance within us.

3. We can ask God to teach and equip us through the Spirit, even in our mundane daily activities.

4. Read about examples of faith in people like Smith Wigglesworth, Brother Lawrence, Madam Guyon, etc. Measure everything you hear by the Word of God.

5. Creating a consciousness of His Presence starts with recognising that He is always with us. He is available for us to talk with and listen to 24/7. Don't switch off your God-consciousness. He is with you.

We pray 'Holy Spirit, come', yet Jesus says that He will never leave us nor forsake us. Holy Spirit is already here. We need to wake up to His continual Presence or run the risk of waiting for the Holy Spirit like we wait for a bus. The Holy Spirit is already on you, around you, and within you.

'We need to wake up to the Presence and live with daily expectation.' *Word of Wisdom*

Compartmentalisation is a big issue for today. We have busy schedules around which we try to fit God, but He is the schedule, the purpose, the way, the truth, the life.

In a recent training session, we as participants were encouraged to spend an hour a day in prayer. I wondered why the other 23 hours weren't a call to prayer, too. If we walk in the Spirit, we walk out of the world and away from a compartmentalised lifestyle.

Talk with and listen to the Spirit of the Father, the Spirit of Jesus: The Holy Spirit.

CHAPTER 10 – KNOW YOUR IDENTITY

Post Resurrection Lifestyle

> *'Be perfect, therefore, as your Heavenly Father is perfect.' Matthew 5:48*

The finished work of the Cross is perfection for you and me. As Mary Poppins might say: 'You're practically perfect!' Except that, you are perfect because of Jesus.

"Hang on!' I hear you cry, 'I'm so not perfect.'

This is a matter of perception. If God sees you without blemish and free from accusation, who are you to say you aren't perfect? The carnal mind has a perception and vast history detailing exactly who it thinks you are. This history and store case of knowledge will frequently point to who you believe you are, which isn't likely to be the whole truth.

Who Jesus really is, is who you really are

Don't go on a self-help journey to discover who you are. The news about you isn't great, which is why Jesus saved you. Go instead on a journey of discovering who Jesus is. To know Jesus is to discover your true identity.

> **'You discover who you are, through discovering who Jesus is.'** *Word of Wisdom*

Another question may be, are new Christians being effectively nurtured into the Kingdom? How much emphasis are we placing on the transforming power of the Holy Spirit?

When I am teaching groups, I jokingly say, 'Of course, you all know that I'm perfect?!'

An awkward, embarrassed or difficult silence usually follows, from people who know me and from people who don't, or some folk might just laugh. But no matter how provocative this statement is on the surface; Scripture says I am redeemed by the Cross; a new creation in Christ. The old is gone and the new has come. Every day is a fresh, happy birthday when you know Jesus.

You see, several Scriptures record God's promise to provide us with a new heart and a new spirit. We just need to believe it.

> *"'I will give you a new heart and put a new spirit in you; I will remove from you your heart of stone and give you a heart of flesh. And I will put my Spirit in you and move you to follow my decrees and be careful to keep my laws.'" Ezekiel 36:26-27*

We even have the mind of Christ. A mind so different to the flesh which is often caught in rebellion and sickness and fracture. We have so much to learn and *unlearn* about who we really are.

> **'Our identity is our inheritance. So often we ask God for what our true identity in Jesus already owns.'** *Word of Wisdom*

The kings of Israel and Judah who did not go awry are described as following the Lord 'whole heartedly.' Otherwise described as 'with their whole hearts.' Without the Holy Spirit in us, for us, this is impossible. We find ourselves caught in Romans 7 (Pre-Holy Spirit living) as opposed to Romans 8 (Spirit filled living), rescued by the Spirit in us. He makes us new.

'To receive the Holy Spirit is to surrender to the Holy Spirit.' *Word of Wisdom*

The clue for surrender is found in Romans 12:1-2. The passage also details the how of transformation.

> *'Therefore, I urge you, brothers and sisters, in view of God's mercy, to offer your bodies as a living sacrifice, holy and pleasing to God—this is your true and proper worship. Do not conform to the pattern of this world, but be transformed by the renewing of your mind.' Romans 12:1-2*

Renewing your mind is the place of understanding and the starting point for transformation. Our opportunity to be transformed is in the renewing of our mind because our understanding of who we are often doesn't fit with a) the Word of God b) God's view of who we truly are.

As an aside, do you remember the books described in Revelation as ready to be opened and read in Heaven?

> *'"And I saw the dead, great and small, standing before the throne, and books were opened. Another book was opened, which is the book of life. The dead were judged according to what they had done as recorded in the books."' Revelation 20:12*

I had dreaded the day my book would be opened in Heaven, in front of great crowds of witnesses, imagining it to be full of hideous sinful crimes, stains and blemishes of disobedience, ignorance and shame (with a few good bits, of course). We don't yet know how our book might read, but the realisation struck me that perhaps my book was a redeemed book. A book full of the good words, thoughts, deeds and examples of goodness, works and fruit secretly and openly carried out over the years. A book redeemed by Jesus.

> *'But now he has reconciled you by Christ's physical body through death to present you holy in his sight, without blemish and free from accusation— if you continue in your faith, established and firm, and do not move from the hope held out in the gospel.' Colossians 1:22-23*

How does Jesus see you? Without blemish? Free from accusation because of Jesus? When does this happen? Paul says, 'But **now**...' Perfected in Jesus. It is done. Complete, yet ongoing. Holy, not pious or religious. Holy, meaning power-full, focused, set apart.

Yet, what is the media view of a Christian stereotype? Nice. Good intentioned. Somewhat out of touch.

SEVEN STEPS FOR FINDING YOUR TRUE IDENTITY

Let's look at seven practical ways through which Jesus learned His identity. How did He become who He was? If we understand how Jesus learned His identity, we can follow His example and become who we *really* are.

What happened during the first 30 years of His life in preparation for His ministry?

1. Jesus Devoured the Word

The Old Testament was a book for Jesus and to Jesus. He read the Old Testament scrolls, which was no mean feat. It is humbling to realise He learned His identity (His potential and reality) through the words of the Old Testament. This is reflected in the New Testament quoting 78 times from Genesis, Exodus, Leviticus, Deuteronomy, Psalms, Proverbs, Isaiah, Jeremiah, Ezekiel, Daniel, Hosea, Amos, Jonah, Micah, and Malachi. Jesus referred to the Old Testament as "the Scriptures," "the word of God," and "the wisdom of God." Jesus said, 'For it is written...' 31 times in the Gospels.

He unrolls a scroll, purported to be at least 24 feet long and around 10 inches high, with 54 columns of unpunctuated text, and declares:

> *"The Spirit of the Lord is on me, because he has anointed me to proclaim good news to the poor.*
> *He has sent me to proclaim freedom for the prisoners and recovery of sight for the blind,*
> *to set the oppressed free,*
> *to proclaim the year of the Lord's favour."* Then he rolled up the scroll, gave it back to the attendant and sat down. The eyes of everyone in the synagogue were fastened on him. He began by saying to them, "Today this Scripture is fulfilled in your hearing."' Luke 4:18 – 21

Jesus doesn't have a concordance, and He doesn't consult a search engine. He simply opens the scroll and finds the place where it is written! Jesus devoured Scripture.

He used it against His enemy. Interestingly, His enemy tried to use it against Him.

'Your life is the fulfilment of Scripture.' *Word of Wisdom*

We read in the Spirit. We read with the Spirit. We find ourselves in the Word of God. Let's devour it, too.

> **'Who you are is found in His promises.'** *Word of Wisdom*

2. *Jesus Cultivated Intimacy with His Father*

Time and again, Jesus took Himself away to solitary places to commune with His Dad. We read that He 'prayed', and yet we don't know the format He used (petition, intercession, silence, listening, being, and so on). Possibly all of these.

> *'Very early in the morning, while it was still dark, Jesus got up, left the house and went off to a solitary place, where he prayed.',Mark 1:35.*

> *'One of those days Jesus went out to a mountainside to pray, and spent the night praying to God.' Luke 6:12.*

> *'After he had dismissed them, he went up on a mountainside by himself to pray. Later that night, he was there alone...' Matthew 14:23*

By bringing ourselves into God's Presence, we are changed into His likeness.

> **'Intimacy comes from trust; trust comes from knowledge; knowledge comes from experience; experience comes from His Presence.'** *Word of Wisdom*

Jesus pursued His Father in all circumstances. At the time of most pressure and darkness, He pursues His father in the garden of Gethsemane. On the Cross, it's His Father He speaks with. Are we pursuing God wholeheartedly? If we aren't, the alternative can only be half-heartedness.

What must we surrender? Are we cultivating intimacy through time in His Presence? Is time something we can give Him, swapping our agenda for His?

3. *Jesus Became His Identity*

Our identity informs everything we do. What we believe about ourselves informs the way we live. Jesus was in no doubt as to who He was. We read the 'I am' statements in the gospel of John Chapter 8, where Jesus details His identity. These aren't the 'I DO' statements. They describe a permanent state of being from which He delivers His purpose.

The Eight 'I Am' statements from Jesus in the Gospel of John

6:35	I am the bread of life
8:12	I am the light of the world
8:58	Before Abraham was, I am
10:9	I am the door
10:11	I am the good shepherd
11:25	I am the resurrection and the life
14:6	I am the way, the truth, and the life
15:1	I am the true vine

Interestingly, we can claim the two 'You are' statements given to us by Jesus, and use them to know our identity and mission. You were born to be where you are now, to make a difference, to be Jesus in this place at this hour.

In Matthew 5:13-16, we read:

> ***'You are the salt of the earth.*** *But if the salt loses its saltiness, how can it be made salty again? It is no longer good for anything, except to be thrown out and trampled underfoot.*

> ***'You are the light of the world.*** *A town built on a hill cannot be hidden. Neither do people light a lamp and put it under a bowl. Instead they put it on its stand, and it gives light to everyone in the house. In the same way, let your light shine before others, that they may see your good deeds and glorify your Father in Heaven.*

This is about our position in the world, our difference, if you like. The word 'glorify' used above *(doxazo)* means to show off. We're supposed to show God off. Salt is either salty or it isn't. Light is light or it isn't light.

'From our being flows our doing.' *Word of Wisdom*

What lies do we need to give up to accept what Jesus says about us? He doesn't say we will become salt and light. He says we already are.

Look at Moses, one of the most broken individuals on earth who, after surrendering to the Lord, becomes one of the most powerful and influential men this planet has ever known. Identity reinforces behaviour. Identity is belief followed by an action. What I believe about who I am leads me to behave according to my beliefs.

'You are who He says you are.' *Word of Wisdom*

'Only believe,' Jesus says.

4. *Jesus Walked in His Purpose*

> '.. and the scroll of the prophet Isaiah was handed to him. Unrolling it, he found the place where it is written: "The Spirit of the Lord is on me, because he has anointed me to proclaim good news to the poor. He has sent me to proclaim freedom for the prisoners and recovery of sight for the blind, to set the oppressed free, to proclaim the year of the Lord's favour." Then he rolled up the scroll, gave it back to the attendant and sat down. The eyes of everyone in the synagogue were fastened on him. He began by saying to them, "Today this Scripture is fulfilled in your hearing."' Luke 4:17-21

Jesus lived out an identity founded on God's Word. He literally lived what He read. We are no different. Let's live it.

5. *Jesus Worked His Inheritance*

> 'Then Jesus came to them and said, "All authority in Heaven and on earth has been given to me. Therefore, go and make disciples of all nations, baptizing them in the name of the Father and of the Son and of the Holy Spirit, and teaching them to obey everything I have commanded you. And surely, I am with you always, to the very end of the age."' Matthew 28:18-20

Jesus used and passed the authority He was given to others. His inheritance wasn't simply an inherited and unused static gift. He picks up His inheritance, declares and uses it! We can do the same.

'His commission is your commission.' *Word of Wisdom*

6. *Jesus Trusted the Plan*

In the natural, Jesus' life didn't look successful. He made enemies. He went hungry. Many doubted His authenticity and mocked Him. His life wasn't that easy. When we look at great Biblical heroes with big destinies, their lives may not appear terribly successful either.

> **'From great struggles, great triumphs arise.'** *Word of Wisdom*

> *"'Father, if you are willing, take this cup from me; yet not my will, but yours be done.'" Luke 22:42*

Trust the plan. If you are pursuing Him, with your hopes and desires resting in His palm; if you are looking to Heaven for wisdom, guidance, and even positioning; trust Him to lead you. He plans to prosper you, not to harm you, even when circumstances appear completely awry. You can trust Him. He is good.

'It is done,' Jesus said. Trust Him.

> **'The more we understand who He is, the more we can become.'** *Word of Wisdom*

7. *Jesus Partnered with Heaven*

> *"After this, Jesus, knowing that all things were now accomplished, that the Scripture might be fulfilled, said, "I thirst!" Now a vessel full of sour wine was sitting there; and they filled a sponge with sour wine, put it on hyssop, and put it to His mouth. So when Jesus had received the sour wine, He said, "It is finished!" And bowing His head, He gave up His spirit." John 19:28-30*

> **'Everything we believe about Who He is and who we are (identity) releases us to live now in the fullness of the Spirit.'** *Word of Wisdom*

The Holy Spirit allows us to partner with Heaven. No longer just as followers of Jesus, but as friends. Co-workers. Colleagues. Co-conspirators. Correspondents. Co-dependants.

Talk with and listen to the Spirit of the Father, the Spirit of Jesus: The Holy Spirit.

CHAPTER 11 – CHOOSING PROPHETIC VISION

Look Through the Kingdom Lens of Love

In a fallen world, where so much is wrong around us, it can be difficult not to have a tainted view of those known and unknown to us. The age-old saying seems to ring true: 'Familiarity breeds contempt.' The more we seem to know someone, the less perfect we find them.

However, from a Kingdom perspective, love breeds respect.

It's easy to scrutinise the foibles of friends, family and self—mistakes, omissions, life choices, aspirations, the have-not-dones and the want-to-dos—to make negative judgements and formulate a tainted picture. How many people do you perceive as perfect?

We cannot insult another person more than to assume that we know them. When we think we know a person, we box them into a perspective from which we rarely allow them to change. The same is true of God. That is why the search for Him is deep and endless while we are on earth. Let's lay aside our preconceptions of God and one another, and allow for growth, connection, positivity, and fresh perspective.

> **'Choosing to see the best in people liberates us to find the best in people.'** *Word of Wisdom*

It was hard to juggle whether to put this Chapter on prophetic vision before or after the Chapter on identity. Our identity informs us of who we are. A strong and true identity will also inform us about who other people are, too.

I have two friends who are just perfect. The husband is beautiful, wise, learned, and decisive. Decisiveness is one of his strengths. One day, several of us were flying out to a Conference in Canada. My married friends were hoping to bump into their close friends on the same flight, but Annie and Nigel could not be found. It was peak flight time and Heathrow was absolutely packed. It was difficult to find space, let alone, sit. Having circled around looking for them, we decided to stop in a large, crowded coffee lounge. Her husband headed to the queue to purchase drinks, leaving me and his wife to find a table.

I caught a glimpse of three seats at an empty table and made a beeline for them with my friend. Her husband saw where we were headed and waved us away.

'Not there,' he said, pointing with some frustration (the place was hot, busy and crowded) to a table across the hall, with less space, it appeared, than the one I had identified. I didn't see my friend with prophetic vision in that moment. Why did he want us to vacate the empty table and wade through the multitudes to the other side? Nonetheless, we went across obediently, asking the couple sitting to one side if we could sit down.

'Yes,' they said. They were waiting for friends.

I sat down, quietly cross. *Why this table and not the other?* Then I overheard the couple on the next table chatting.

'What did she say?'

'She is booked onto the 2:50 flight to Toronto and going to the same event.' My flight was at 2.50p.m. too!

Their chat continued. 'And where are they now?'

'Well, I have just seen Annie in WH Smith, and Nigel is heading over in 5 minutes.'

I blinked. An Annie and a Nigel? Could it be possible?

'Excuse me,' I said, 'I couldn't help over-hearing your conversation, but are you going to the Conference in Toronto, and your friends are Annie and Nigel from Cambridge?'

'Yes,' she replied, obviously curious.

Shortly after this, Annie and Nigel arrived to sit next to my two friends who had been searching for them for some time! What an extraordinary thing in this expanse of airport, people and busyness! Had we sat where I originally chosen to sit, we might not have found Annie and Nigel before flying. God had used my friend's decisiveness to direct us to the right place to sit.

'Seeing people as God sees them is to view people through the Kingdom lens of love.'
Word of Wisdom

In relation to prophetic vision, Peter and his relationship with Jesus is fascinating. Was Peter a great hero of faith?

Prior to Jesus' resurrection we see Peter being fearful, lacking in understanding, and used as the enemy's mouthpiece. He could be viewed as a traitor, coward, jealous of others in ministry, competitive, likely had an inferiority complex and needed to prove himself. Peter is all of these things. Do you know anyone like this? So human it hurts? Perhaps you see one or two of these traits in yourself, and have even ruled yourself out because of these imperfections? Hurt people, hurt people, as someone once said.

One of Peter's biggest and most glaring pre-resurrection errors happened during the transfiguration of Jesus.

> 'After six days Jesus took with him Peter, James and John the brother of James, and led them up a high mountain by themselves. There he was transfigured before them. His face shone like the sun, and his clothes became as white as the light. Just then there appeared before them Moses and Elijah, talking with Jesus. Peter said to Jesus, "Lord, it is good for us to be here. If you wish, I will put up three tents—one for you, one for Moses and one for Elijah." While he was still speaking, a bright cloud covered them, and a voice from the cloud said, "This is my Son, whom I love; with him I am well pleased. Listen to him!" Matthew 17:1-5

This was a powerful and holy moment. Imagine the weight of the Presence of God as a cloud covers them. Moses and Elijah are talking with Jesus, and Peter, clumsy in the moment and unable to keep the silence blurts out;

'I will put up three tents.' Right at the point when the Father speaks to His Son from Heaven! He almost ruins the moment.

Then in Matthew 16, we see this flash of brilliance and potential in Peter when Jesus asks His disciples,

'Who do people say I am?'

From all the dud responses, Peter reveals the fullness of Jesus' identity in his reply: 'You are the Christ, the Son of the living God'.

> "And I tell you that you are Peter, and on this rock I will build my church, and the gates of Hades will not overcome it." Matthew 16:18

When Jesus first meets him, He establishes Peter's prophetic identity by declaring his name: *Cephas*, or rock. He doesn't treat Peter as He finds him. He doesn't judge Peter based on his shortcomings. He sees Peter from Heaven's perspective as 'the rock.' Prophetic vision. It's how Jesus sees us. Can we do the same with each other?

> **'We need to use the eyes of love and not the eyes of judgement.'** *Word of Wisdom*

Peter must be encouraged by Jesus' public affirmation of his role and purpose in the Church. That declaration must fill Peter with new-found self-respect and confidence. So, how does he get it so wrong, just two verses later? Has he become over-confident because of the weight of Jesus' prophetic declaration into his life?

Jesus is warning the disciples about the things that need to happen for His mission on earth to be fulfilled. He must be killed and raised to life on the third day. Peter, once again, clumsy in the flesh and not in the Spirit (there is a vast difference between the two), appears to become overfamiliar and unwise with Jesus. In effect, among other things, Peter tells Jesus He hasn't heard correctly from His Father.

> *Peter took him aside and began to rebuke him. "Never, Lord!" he said. "This shall never happen to you!" Jesus turned and said to Peter, "Get behind me, Satan! You are a stumbling block to me; you do not have in mind the concerns of God, but merely human concerns."*
> *Matthew 16:22-23*

From public affirmation to public rebuke. It must have been painful for Peter to experience those words, but Jesus wasn't being flippant or name calling. He recognised that His adversary the devil was trying to deter Him from His destiny as Saviour.

Give Love A-Way

But even though Peter got it so horribly wrong, he was still *the rock*. His name, Cephas, is the label. He didn't suddenly change and God didn't change His mind about Peter and his role in history. God sees us through the eyes of love.

What was Peter's potential? After all his failings, shortcomings and mistakes, we see him after the resurrection, a transformed man. After the first infilling of the Spirit, this same Peter, who publicly denied Jesus three times, witnesses to over 3000 people! That's 1000 people for each denial!

Peter is not reinstated. He was never demoted. The Holy Spirit brings about the same radical transformation in Peter that will be worked in us as we are filled with the Spirit and allow the Lord to be the Lord in our lives, too.

> **'We pray "thy will be done"; not "my will be done".'** *Word of Wisdom*

Those very flesh-like and human characteristics that Peter displayed prior to the resurrection became the foundation for the future. From fear to courage; from lacking understanding to wise; from mouthpiece of the enemy to mouthpiece of God; from coward to champion; from traitor to true; from inferiority to boldness; from jealousy of others to facilitating growth in others; from competitive to surrendered.

The enemy will often blow his cover by going that step too far, thus revealing his strategy to destroy.

What was the primary negative issue for you as a child? For me, a fear of people and large groups. Why, in a spiritual sense, was this the case? Because it is always my destiny to speak with people and converse with groups. Either the enemy used fear to try to destroy me and God used this weapon fashioned against me to prosper me. Or, the enemy foresaw a destiny and tried to destroy it. Or both.

Either way, the Lord can and will use our brokenness, shortcomings and history, when we surrender ourselves back to Him.

Let us say: Holy Spirit, take me, use me.

Every time we minister out on the streets, the words we receive and convey from God to Pre-Christians are loving, kind, encouraging, insightful, wise, faith-building and brilliant. This is a God who believes in potential; in you, me and others. He personifies the love described in 1 Corinthians 13. He doesn't treat us as our sins deserve. There is no rebuke, instead, He extends the voice and hand of infinite love. God doesn't set Himself up as above us all, but seeks to lift us out of our pit of selfishness with all its negative repercussions. Can we do the same?

Can we look at a tattoo and describe it with words of love, and not judgement? Can we lay down our judgements of others and breathe in the fullness of the Holy Spirit? Lord, I surrender.

Let's look at the most shocking and revealing prophetic vision: the way the Lord sees His Church – the Bride. This is the best illustration of prophetic vision (and prophetic heart).

> 'Husbands, love your wives, just as Christ loved the
> church and gave himself up for her to make her
> holy, cleansing her by the washing with water through
> the word, and to present her to himself as a radiant
> church, without stain or wrinkle or any other blemish,
> but holy and blameless.' Ephesians 5:25-27

A church without blemish? Do I think about my church the same way? Do I see your church the way Jesus sees it? Blameless, holy? We sometimes find it easy to criticise the Bride of Christ when Jesus clearly loves His Bride and views her as perfect.

Only prophetic vision can catch us up into beauty, and transform the imperfect into the perfect and beautiful.

When will we stop judging one another's character and see through the eyes of grace and love? One of the saddest developments in the Kingdom today is the Christians who publicly 'expose' servants of Jesus as 'heretics' (or worse). We can find these prolific modern 'media inquisitions' on Facebook, Twitter and YouTube. Paul faced the same issues of judgement in his day and writes about this in 1 Corinthians 4.

Even Jesus' acts of love, grace and mercy, were deemed as working for the enemy by the religious and self-righteous. Can we take the narrow, more difficult route of Kingdom *building*, as opposed to seeking to destroy others? Let's be generous in our theology and allow God to judge. Who is to say that I am right and you are wrong, or vice versa? One day we may know, when the One True Judge meets us. Perhaps He will be more concerned about how we have loved.

Let the one who earned the right to judge have His rightful place.

Prophetic vision allows us to pray with eyes of faith. One of the best examples can be found with Joshua in the Old Testament.

> *'On the day the LORD gave the Amorites over to Israel, Joshua said to the LORD in the Presence of Israel: "Sun, stand still over Gibeon, and you, moon, over the Valley of Aijalon." So the sun stood still, and the moon stopped, till the nation avenged itself on its enemies, as it is written in the Book of Jashar. The sun stopped in the middle of the sky and delayed going down about a full day. There has never been a day like it before or since, a day when the LORD listened to a human being. Surely the LORD was fighting for Israel!' Joshua 10:12-14*

God didn't tell Joshua to command the sun to stand still and the moon to stop. Joshua stepped out. It's worth remembering at this point that Joshua spent his childhood and youth serving Moses in the tent while Moses chatted with God face to face, like a friend (Exodus 33).

'We must find intimacy before we find power.' *Word of Wisdom*

Then there is Elijah, one of the most powerful prophets in the Bible. I find his actions intriguing, often raising more questions than answers.

For example, we first encounter him in 1 Kings 17, declaring to King Ahab of Israel that there would be no dew or rain for the next few years, except at Elijah's word. After this, the Lord instructs Elijah to leave, presumably because of the risk to his life from the Israelites.

Does God command or direct Elijah to release this 'no rain' declaration to Ahab? Or, like Joshua, does this utterance come from faith in the power of the spoken word and in the God who responds to our requests? You may wonder why this matters.

Let's look at what Jesus tells us about the prayer of faith:

> *'He replied, ".... Truly I tell you, if you have faith as small as a mustard seed, you can say to this mountain, 'Move from here to there,' and it will move. Nothing will be impossible for you."' Matthew 17:20*

Through prophetic prayer, we speak our heart's desires into being. It's the prayer God taught Ezekiel, a man who had frequent encounters with the Holy Spirit. In Ezekiel 37:1-3, Ezekiel says:

> *"The hand of the Lord was on me, and he brought me out by the Spirit of the Lord and set me in the middle of a valley; it was full of bones. He led me back and forth among them, and I saw a great many bones on the*

> *floor of the valley, bones that were very dry. He asked me, "Son of man, can these bones live?" I said, "O Sovereign Lord, you alone know."'*

After this, the Lord instructs him to prophesy to the bones and issue prophetic declarations clothing the bones with tendons, flesh, skin and breath. God teaches him the value of prophetic vision, seeing what is dead as an opportunity for life, what is rotten as an opportunity for good, what is evil as an opportunity for Heaven to reign. Prophetic prayers clothe the hopeless situation or person with words of life, healing and restoration.

Do you see a cashier at the checkout as your shopping passes down the conveyor belt, or do you see a potential evangelist, pastor, prophet, or teacher for the Kingdom? How does God see this person?

We must wake up to the people around us.

I'm just learning to stretch and extend faith through declarations in the Spirit. How do you know you're in the Spirit? By staying connected to the consciousness of God in, around and on you. Have you ever tapped a crystal vase or glass? The beautiful pitch from the crystal resonates with clarity. So it is when we are in step with the Spirit. Jesus walked in this same clarity in the Spirit.

Some of us need to forgive and stop judging ourselves by our past 'failures'. We all need to forgive and stop judging others by their failures. Prophetic vision chooses to love in all circumstances. This doesn't mean that we don't obey God, or even that we act foolishly. There are one or two people from whom I occasionally distance myself because their prickly fruit can be piercing. They still belong to the Lord. They are still mighty for the Kingdom.

> **'We have an audience of one; let's live to please Him.'** *Word of Wisdom*

Prophetic vision for ourselves must spring from our identity in Jesus. What do you see when you look in the mirror? A failure? A loser? An outcast? Let's take a look at identity now in order to learn further to see ourselves, and others, with the eyes of Heaven. Ask Jesus, 'How do you see me?' Wait for a sense of what He says about you. What He says will be truth.
Prophetic vision, or the belief in the impossible, will always equip us to step out in ordinary situations and leave responsibility with God to answer.

Lunchtime, and I pulled into Sainsburys' car park which was packed with cars and shoppers. As I got out of my car, a young guy was poking a metal rod into a car window about three cars ahead, as if he was trying to unlock the door. A woman was watching with her arms folded beside a car full of young people. Other people stood milling around.

Was everything okay? I wondered, but not enough to stop. I headed inside to buy my lunch and groceries.

Twenty-five minutes later, I returned to my car. The guy was still sticking an implement into a very closed window. He looked frustrated. The young woman was now on her phone and peering into the back of the car. I realised she was locked out of her car and her friends had turned up to help.

That week, I had learned that Jesus was led by compassion whenever He healed anyone. I felt compassion for the young woman standing helpless by her locked car. What did I have that might help? Faith in a miracle-working Expert in solutions and unlocking doors? I also had keys. A spiritual key in Jesus, and a physical key to my car.

'Lord,' I said under my breath, 'can you open this door for this young woman?'

> **'Prayers of faith do not generally say "please".**
> **They are more likely to say "thank you".'** *Word of Wisdom*

It wasn't my best prayer. God and the question 'can you?' are not a good faith combination. But it was all I had. It was a huge risk, but prophetic vision enabled me to believe my car key could open hers. Because of Jesus!

I went over. 'Excuse me,' I said, waggling my car key in the air. 'I think this key will open the door. In fact, I know it can.'

(Prophetic activation. *Come on, Jesus! I'm stepping out!*)

'Go ahead.' The young lad said, stepping back.

I have to tell you that I wasn't full of faith. To be a witness and take a risk would have been to tell the group:

'I prayed Jesus would open your car door using this key.' But I didn't say this, just in case the door didn't open. I lacked the faith.

I inserted the key as everyone watched. Only half a centimetre went into the lock. I groaned inwardly.

'Jesus, please! Jesus, please!' I muttered under my breath, wiggling the key just a fraction. Everyone watched. Nothing happened. I tried again. Still nothing.

I stepped back. 'Oh, well. It was worth a try.' I said, disappointed.

The young man smiled sympathetically.

One more time. I thought. *Jesus, you can do it!*

I stepped back up, put the key back in the lock and wiggled the key one more time. Right before our eyes, the locks on all four doors popped up! The young woman gasped, her friends laughed, and now was the time for testimony (albeit late!)

'Excuse me, 'I said. I didn't tell you this, but I'm a Christian and I love Jesus. I asked Him to unlock your car door with my key and He just did.'

They looked back and forth at each other like I was an alien (I am). As I walked away, I heard one of them say, 'She's got a key that *can unlock any door*!' Technically, spiritually correct, but in the natural, incorrect!

Laughing, I turned round. 'It wasn't my key that unlocked the door. I asked Jesus to do it.'

Sowing seeds. People matter. Stay switched on.

Talk with and listen to the Spirit of the Father, the Spirit of Jesus: The Holy Spirit.

CHAPTER 12 – REACHING OUT THROUGH THE HOLY SPIRIT

New Possibilities for Us All

> *'Do not be conformed to this world, but be transformed by the renewal of your mind, that by testing you may discern what is the will of God, what is good and acceptable and perfect.' Romans 12:2*

Our traditional views of evangelism don't always help us. A new perspective allows for new possibilities.

Evangelism is probably the least understood, and least aspired to, of all the spiritual gifts. Anyone remotely brave enough to mention Jesus to a Pre-Christian might quickly be labelled an evangelist by the general church population. An evangelist is perceived as a brave risk taker. In reality, with a new understanding of what evangelism really is, outreach or reaching out to others becomes easy and natural, and requires no exceptional bravery or gift. It becomes normal life.

My purpose in writing this book comes from having been labelled an evangelist because I talk to others about Jesus.

Having been broken and subsequently rescued by Jesus—from death to life, and fear to strength—I now know how to love people. Love is the purest form of outreach or evangelism. We are all equipped to love, and love looks like God. Everyone deserves an encounter with God before they die. You are that encounter waiting to happen.

> **'Instead of waiting for the divine appointment, you are the divine appointment.'**
> *Word of Wisdom*

Since we know how to love because God loves us back to life in Him, unwrapping what evangelism is and isn't becomes vital to understanding how to reach out to others, and creates new potential for success in sharing Jesus.

> **'Evangelism is often perceived as easy for people with 'the gift', but an often-impossible challenge for those without 'the gift.''**
> *Word of Wisdom*

I recently heard a world-renowned Christian leader say, 'I'm so glad that I don't have to do evangelism. It's just not my gift.'

Comments like the following are common. I used many myself before my employment as Outreach Lead:

- 'It's not for me.'
- 'I don't have that gift.'
- 'It's not my calling.'
- 'I wouldn't know how to do it.'
- 'I wouldn't know what to say.'
- 'What if they ask a question I can't answer?'
- 'I'm not brave enough.'
- 'I'm not called to speak non-Christians. My calling is to Christians.'
- 'I have a teaching/pastoral/prophetic gift. Evangelism isn't my role.'
- 'We shouldn't force the gospel down people's throats.'
- 'I don't know any non-Christians.'
- 'Religion is private.'

A recent Church survey encapsulates many of our misunderstandings and misconceptions about evangelism. In the general comments section, a church member wrote: 'The relentless push to bring new people into the church stinks of commercialism'.

A 'relentless push' seems to criticise and condemn the very purpose for which we are saved by Jesus. Were you ever in need of rescue by Jesus? Do you remember the pain of being lost? A great motivator for sharing Jesus is love. Loving the other enough to introduce them, in any small way, to the great Lover.

If we each win one person a year to Jesus, the Church doubles in size each year. And if we don't become a witness for Jesus, who will stand as salt and light for the lost?

'I haven't got time to evangelise', I once said to God, because I understood evangelism as something I did, not someone I am. Evangelism carried that nagging sense of guilt. Anything else looked more appealing than going cold turkey and speaking to people to 'who should know better' about Jesus. That day, I rushed around the house, trying to get 50 things done in one hour, including a shopping trip. I hopped into the car, and as I tore around the store focused on groceries, I suddenly heard the unmistakable, quiet, fearsome voice of God.

'Open your eyes. This IS the mission field.'

Those words transformed my thinking like a sledgehammer. We need answers to the issues surrounding our understanding evangelism because we then become a solution for people who need to encounter a living Jesus.

'When we understand what evangelism is and what evangelism isn't, out-reach becomes full of possibilities.' *Word of Wisdom*

When considering the word 'evangelism', instead of good news, many might think of the discomfort or embarrassment; stepping over boundaries into someone else's world; encountering people who may not be interested, or worse, become angry when we 'cold call' our views.

Somehow, I had confused evangelism with feeling awkward, dreading the questions I couldn't answer, and trying to 'do it right'. I was doing it through tense moral obligation rather than out of love and peace.

'Evangelism' (giving of good news) and 'proselytising' (attempting to convert people to faith) can be easily confused. Historical (and sometimes current) evangelism modelled a 'them and us' confrontation, with threats of fear and judgement for those 'outside' the faith.

'We can confuse church with 'a building', and the walls in our buildings can keep the Christians in and the 'non-Christians' out.' *Word of Wisdom*

Church becomes a place we go to, rather than **two or three gathered in His name** (Matthew 18:20). We know this because we routinely talk about being at, or going to church on a Sunday, when actually, we are going to a building in which we *are* the church. Two or three gathered in His name is Church.

Why does this make a difference? Because our walls so easily create a 'them and us' mentality. This in itself is Biblical, because we are aliens and strangers in this world once we follow Jesus, and, technically, we are from a different Kingdom to the rest of humankind. However, being an alien doesn't mean that we should *alienate* ourselves or others from knowing Jesus, the God of Love. We can't let our walls keep people out, or lead us to believe a building is our best home.

The building can be a great resource to meet with and minister to people. However, we have waited too long for people to visit our buildings and stopped recognising that, when Jesus said 'Go', He really meant it. Go isn't fulfilled by waiting for people to come to us. Jesus sent out the twelve, followed by the seventy-two. The mandate for each disciple then and now is to go and make disciples of all nations; to lay hands on the sick, free the captives and bind up the broken hearted.

If I do not have a pastoral gift, can I love others like I want to be loved? Or lead by example without a teaching gift? Without a prophetic anointing, can I prophesy? The answer is yes. Likewise, spreading the good news is not exclusive to those with the evangelist's gift. Love encompasses all the gifts and looks like outreach. We can all love by reaching out to others.

My family, rather irritatingly but truthfully, reflect on the time I became a Christian many years ago, full of zeal and passionate to share my new-found God experience. They say I turned from a lovely person into a nasty one. It was me against them. I was saved and they weren't, so 'they' became my enemy. In life's great pecking order, I was found, they were lost; I was right and they were wrong.

> **'We can create divides through our lack of love, when love is the bridge to encountering Jesus.'** *Word of Wisdom*

The notion of Christian versus non-Christian is another barrier to building bridges for people to enter the Kingdom. A better term for those who don't yet know Jesus might be Pre-Christian, on the assumption that we want everyone to encounter and have a relationship with Jesus. Pre-Christians are on a journey to encounter Jesus; after all, He died for everyone. Let's take down the 'them' and 'us'; 'we-are-righter-than-them' barriers. After all, as the Word says:

> *'...all have sinned and fall short of the glory of God...'*
> Romans 3:23

We all need a Saviour – those who know Jesus now, those who don't, or may never know Him on this planet.

> **'We must first define what evangelism is.'**
> *Word of Wisdom*

Our actions flow from our mindset. Understanding evangelism is the starting point for transformed thinking and action.

Evangelism is not:

- A spiritual gift that some have but most of us don't
- Something others who are called to it 'do'
- An intellectual exercise or approach we have to get right
- Awkward, uncomfortable, or difficult
- A set time and place
- Something only brave people do
- A task for extraverts
- An obligation
- An intrusion into privacy
- Offensive
- A skill or an art
- Something for full time missionaries or evangelists

Evangelism is:

- A call to look like love in everyday places
- Someone you are, not something you must do
- Choosing to treat someone like they matter
- Seeing beyond the ordinary to the extraordinary
- A response to His love for you, in you
- An over-flow from the in-flow of His love
- Your representation of who Jesus is on this planet
- Making every person count
- Seeing the world as God sees it
- Living for His agenda

> **'Wherever you are, evangelism is.'** *Word of Wisdom*

These concepts developed over many years of personal failure, trying and change. Each of us can practice a lifestyle of looking like love; be conscious of walking in love, in Jesus, in the Spirit.

Points to reflect on

- You are one of the greatest gifts to the world
- Your life is the revelation of Jesus on this planet today
- You carry God's Presence, which means all things are possible through you
- You are in a process of transformation
- Transformation comes through revelation, not explanation
- Your life is a message sent by Heaven to the world,
- The Word of God contains the DNA needed to inform you about who you really are
- Where you are, love is

Talk with and listen to the Spirit of the Father, the Spirit of Jesus: The Holy Spirit.

CHAPTER 13 – STICKING PLASTERS ON LEPERS

Chocolates, Dreams, Tattoos and Streets

This chapter is like a smorgasbord of outreach ideas, stories, lessons learned and tips to utilise as you step out and reach out to others through 'looking like love'.

The Secret of Effective Evangelism

I went to a Conference and attended a 'Masterclass on Outreach' with Blaine Cook, one of my spiritual heroes. Pen poised, notepad in hand and leaning forward in my seat, all my attention was focused. I was so ready to learn, so hungry to find out how to share the gospel.

'You're here for a masterclass in evangelism and how to do it.' Blaine said. 'Here it is.' He leaned forward conspiratorially on the lectern, and looked intently at us all. After a long pause, he quietly said,

'Talk to unbelievers.'

Then a very long silence. I blinked.

'That's it,' he said. 'Go out and mix with unbelievers. Talk to people who don't know Jesus. You'll be amazed at what happens when you pray for them,'

It was as simple as that.

Evangelism isn't rocket science. We mix with Pre-Christians every day, at work, at home, in the supermarket, outside the school gate. As we walk, park, arrive, and depart. Pre-Christians are everywhere around you.

> **'Outreach is everywhere you are. Where you are, outreach is.'** *Word of Wisdom*

Your Story is His-Story

Like Moses, you have a testimony. It doesn't have to be a dramatic story about murder or a turnaround. Perhaps you grew up in a Christian family, had an idyllic childhood, a stable job, a relationship that never failed, and attended a church weekly with no real issues. You still have a story.

> In a world struggling with anxiety, do you have peace?
> In a world where millions are afraid of death, are you unafraid?
> In a world where millions live with the uncertainty of financial lack, do you trust in God?
> In a world where guilt destroys, are you forgiven?
> In a world where bad news fills our media, do you know the good news?
> In a world in fear of the future, do you have certainty?

If you have a relationship with Jesus, you have a story. It doesn't need drama to make it more real. And if you don't feel you have a story (which you do), let Jesus tell His story through signs and wonders. Step out with: 'Can I pray for you?'

I took to carrying my testimony around on an A4 Letter. Whenever I am out and about or running errands, I give my A4 letter to someone I feel prompted to approach. Or, if someone steps into my space and initiates a conversation, I offer them the letter.

'Excuse me, I know this sounds weird,' I explain. 'I felt Jesus prompting me to give you this letter. It's how I became a Christian, my journey. It may mean nothing to you and you can simply throw it away. But here it is anyway.'

Perhaps you could create your own letter or card?

Speak from the Tree of Life

'Love, not judgement.' *Word of Wisdom*

A middle-aged mother of five children stopped at our blackboard in town this week. On our blackboard we have written: 'Dream Interpretation' (it's biblical); and a 'Message from Heaven' (the prophetic).

'Go on, then. Give me a message from Heaven.' She said with a smile.

We explained our love for Jesus, that He communicates with us today. We offered to ask Him for a word, picture, an impression, or a Bible verse, that communicated His love for her.

'Is that ok?' We asked.

Angela said yes.

We explained that we would stand quietly for 2 minutes or so and ask Jesus to speak to us. On this day I was working with a new Christian from my church. She closed her eyes tightly, scrunched her face in concentration and held her hands up in the air.

Reminder: I thought. Teach her that when we pray on the streets, we stand with our eyes open, to avoid looking strange and inaccessible to passers-by. I tend to look at the pavement in order to concentrate.

The picture came quickly. It was a large heart. Angela's hands were somehow trying to reach out from inside the heart. I sensed frustration at trying so hard, but being unable to reach others. The picture then transitioned to Jesus standing alongside Angela.

I looked up and checked in with my team mate that we were ready to share what we felt that we had heard. We shared our pictures with Angela and asked if they resonated with her.

Laughing, she said 'yes', and explained that she had been 'a healer' from a young age and was now a reiki healing practitioner.

My concern here would be that, when we deal with any spirit who is not Holy Spirit, we are at great risk (even likelihood) of opening ourselves up to a spirit world that does not reflect the freedom that comes from Heaven.

At this point, I chose to eat from the tree of life (look like love) and not the tree of the knowledge of good and evil (pronouncing judgement). I explained that, for hundreds of years, the church has kept secret its hidden treasure, called the Holy Spirit. That, to know the Holy Spirit is to receive safe communications from God. That the Holy Spirit equips us with love, joy, peace, patience and so on, as well as the same power Jesus used to heal the sick and raise the dead.

Looking astounded, Angela kept thanking us for the encouragement. She was about to leave when I asked her, 'When you pray, do you feel God is somewhere up there,' I point to the sky, 'or inside here?' I covered my heart with my hand.

This is a great indicator for whether or not someone has a living relationship with Jesus. He lives within us when we invite Him in to our lives.

'I don't know,' she replied. 'Up there somewhere.'

'Would you like to have Jesus in your life?' I continued. 'You can invite Him in. In return, every selfish or hurtful thing you have ever done will be taken on by Him, and today will be like a birthday, a beginning for the rest of your life.'

'I want that,' Angela replied.

I tried to put her off, so that she would know that this is a commitment for life, and not just a day. 'It's a huge commitment, bigger than a wedding day. You're giving everything you are and all that you have to Jesus.'

'I really want that,' she said.

Then I explained that I would lead her in a simple prayer. I stepped out in faith and said that she would feel different afterwards, and would experience the power of God as we prayed.

I led her in a simple prayer of repentance—saying sorry for every wrong she had done in the past, and declaration—a commitment to making Jesus her Lord.

In the middle of the pedestrian walkway, Angela made a commitment to Jesus. She stayed there for a while with her eyes closed, obviously experiencing the strong Presence of God. After a while, she sighed, smiled, and said, 'Wow. I feel like a new born baby!' Yes!

To become a Christian, I told Angela, is to become one of the most powerful people on this planet.

'Which church do you go to?' Angela asked, as she left.

'Kingsland in Colchester.' We replied.

She looked at us in shock. 'Not Kingsland above Aldi in Lexden?'

'Yes.'

'Oh! I've always wanted to visit you all. When I shop at Aldi, I deliberately go upstairs to use your toilets because there is such a lovely feeling up there! I'm going to come with the family on Sunday week, if that's ok?'

To be continued...!

Reading Tattoos on the Streets

Each year, several of the 40-plus churches in Colchester come together and offer a Free Family Fun Festival to the population of Colchester. Everything, except for beverages, is free: donkey rides, games, bouncy castles, face-painting, dog shows, numerous games and stalls provide free entertainment. In 2019 we estimate that around 10,000 people wandered through Castle Park in Colchester. It was such a great opportunity to look like love and give love A-Way.

We also have a Mind, Body, Spirit Team operating to offer a menu of choices, including: Tattoo Reading, Dream Interpretation, Message from Heaven, Peace Experience, Hope Booster, and Healing Prayer. It's so encouraging to have Pre-Christians waiting for ministry in the Holy Spirit. Each intervention is a powerful seed sown, ready for harvest.

Tattoo reading is so interesting. Where possible, I like to train others in looking like love, and sometimes, this happens accidently.

On one occasion at the Free Fun Family Festival, a man walked past me. As you know by now, anyone who steps into my one metre circle (or two, during the COVID-19 period) has entered my territory and is, I believe, probably sent by God. It was September, a fine and sunny day. Because he had a t-shirt on, I could see his tattoos.

Two Christians had just finished talking to me about tattoo reading, pointing out their belief that all tattoos are demonic in nature, and how did I minister to people with tattoos? I talked about looking like love when we reach out, and that there are always positives from the Holy Spirit. The enemy may believe he has marked a person for death, but we know Jesus marks people for life.

Anyhow, the man walks past, I see his tattoos, and call out to him. 'Can I interpret your tattoos, please?'

The Christians I was chatting with were nearby, so when the man agreed, I called them over.

'I hope you don't mind,' I explained, 'but my two friends have been asking how tattoos are interpreted. Can I use this as a teaching session, too?'

The guy was amenable.

I remember asking the Holy Spirit what He wanted to say, based on the design of the tattoos I was seeing. Very often, the Lord will download or infill prophetic words for the person in question.
A minute or so passed as I looked at the skulls, demonic figures, snakes with fangs, etc. When I was ready, I asked the two Christians if God showed them anything.

One of the women stepped back, and frowned. 'No, but they are obviously demonic.'

Hmm. Would this help our man with tattoos?

I don't recall the specific words the Holy Spirit gave me to bless this man, but he left amazed, encouraged and touched. The greater purpose of every intervention is to pray with the person and invite the Spirit to touch and make Himself known to them.

This week, a Christian lady came to check me out as I worked on the street in town. To discern, I guess, and hopefully not to judge.

'Based on what the Bible says, what do you think of tattoos?' She asked.

It was one of those rhetorical questions, because she knew I knew what the Bible says. Yet, I am responsible for teaching the way of love, not judgement. How far would I get if I said to each person I met, 'You're a wretched sinner because of your tattoo! You are breaking the laws of God'?

> *"'Do not cut your bodies for the dead or put tattoo marks on yourselves. I am the Lord.'" Leviticus 19:28*

I explained to the Christian woman that, from what I have seen to date, some tattoos appear demonic in nature. But many don't appear to be dangerous. I explained that Jesus leads with love and wants to pour out His love on people for the sake of grace. John 3:16 does not say: 'For God so *judged* the world that He gave His one and only Son, that whoever believes in Him shall not perish but have eternal life.'

I cheekily suggested to this Christian lady who began with wanting to correct me, that Jesus probably has a tattoo Himself. God can be surprising when we think we have Him boxed!

> *'On his robe and **on his thigh, he has this name written**:*
> KING OF KINGS AND LORD OF LORDS.' Revelation 19:16

'If you look with the eyes of love, you see with the eyes of love.' *Word of Wisdom*

Perhaps my most powerful dream and tattoo-led encounter was with a passing young couple, who stopped to look at the chalkboard one hot summer afternoon.

Clasping her partner's hand, the young woman said, 'Can I have a message from Heaven, please?'

My friend and I explained the process. We love Jesus and believe He loves her, and we would convey any word, picture or sense of Jesus speaking to her.

As I closed my eyes and fixed my thoughts on Jesus, a beautiful mental picture emerged of a tiny paper boat on a wide, fast-flowing river, bobbing downstream towards a destination where people stood in a small group. As the boat went down this river, the young woman called to people on the shore to get into the boat with her, but the impression was that no one wanted to. I felt her sense of sadness and disappointment at being rejected by those 'on the shore'.

The woman and her partner listened intently as I relayed this picture to her. I described the boat (I felt it was her). I described the emotions I sensed when the people she called out to and those on the shore wouldn't get in; essentially rejecting her.

The woman immediately poured her heart out. The picture so accurately reflected her life, she was astonished! She was due to marry her partner in a week and couldn't understand why her relatives were refusing to come to the wedding. The people on the shore, she felt, were her family.

We were able to tell her and her fiancé that Jesus is alive and knows each of them intimately. One of the most notable aspects of the picture Jesus gave was the significance of the number 'five' in this mental picture. I knew the boat arrived at, most likely, a group of five people. The number felt specific.

'Does the number five mean anything to you?' I asked Tom tentatively.
He stared at me quietly, stepped back and held out his big hand like a stop signal in front of my face. There, tattooed on his palm, was the number 5! It was awesome to pray for this young couple, both struck by a God who knew and loved them. They went away connected to Jesus.

We can release life and love to any person we encounter; regardless of tattoos reading 'HATE', or demon-like images burned into the skin. We can mark people for Jesus eternally through releasing words of love and life.

See with prophetic vision. Look with the eyes of love. It is great to see beauty when we choose not to see judgement or condemnation.

Spirit Café – Harvest Ministries

I had heard of a ministry in Birmingham that runs an outreach to the community called 'Spirit Café', offering a menu of ministry options to the public – mostly Pre-Christians – one night a week. Lori Arnott Lawlor heads up this ministry, and they regularly offer training on how Spirit Café works, with an invitation for you to set up your own Spirit Café on completion of the training.

Lori is based in a building which used to be a pub. I travelled up to Birmingham to hear more and investigate, intending to bring these outreach tools back to Colchester. Lori had seen psychics and mediums outreaching and selling services in public places and, knowing the Holy Spirit, she and her team originated the Christian Spirit-led Spirit Café to offer a Holy Spirit reality to people searching for spiritual truth.

A 'compere' meets visitors at the door and offers a menu of 'Treatments'. Visitors can sign up for one or two treatments. Three or four teams of two people are allocated one 'guest' each, and then Jesus is invited in to provide whatever is needed e.g., a 'Spiritual reading', which could be a prophetic word, picture, Scripture, etc., or 'Peace Treatment', where Holy Spirit is invited to bring peace.

It is a beautiful and simple way of introducing Pre-Christians to the realities of a living Jesus, Father and Holy Spirit.

On the evening I attended to observe, around 30 people visited from the local area. It was humbling. When do we get 30 people ready to encounter the spiritual reality of Jesus in a church building, albeit a reconditioned British pub! Several people made a commitment to Jesus for the first time.

The encounter I remember best was a really sceptical woman who arrived with four friends. She didn't believe in God and thought the whole concept was fake rubbish. However, she was there with four friends who participated in treatments and were touched powerfully by the Lord.

The ministry doesn't happen tucked away in a room somewhere. The guests wait in an open room, where the ministry happens at one end and tea and coffee is served in the café area at the other. The lady heard each friend recount their experience and decided—albeit sceptically—to sign up for a Peace Treatment. Unfortunately for her, her encounter with God wasn't quite the experience she might have asked for! The Holy Spirit touched her in such a powerful way that she immediately started laughing. It was not ordinary laughter, but laughter in the Spirit. She laughed so hard that the entire room laughed, too!

'What's happening to me?' she asked. Tears streamed down her face and she actually slid off her chair onto the floor! She was drunk in the Spirit.

'This isn't possible!' She continued. 'I don't even believe in this stuff!' It was truly beautiful to see her touched by the Holy Spirit in that convincing and life changing encounter.

So many search for a spiritual reality in dangerous places like spiritualist meetings, tarot phone lines and contact with fortune tellers. People are hungry for a spiritual reality that they don't realise exists within Christianity. Dealings with a spiritual world that does not involve the Holy Spirit will pollute the receiver spiritually. Only the Holy Spirit brings freedom.

We must discover the Lordship of God in our lives, homes and fellowship meetings. We must become ready to listen and allow Him to lead. The Holy Spirit reveals Jesus to us and makes church alive, vibrant and relevant. Let us free the Holy Spirit to be Lord.

To learn more about Spirit Café, check out Harvest Ministries in Birmingham: www.harvestministries.co.uk. In a world full of counterfeit spirits ready to lie, kill, steal and destroy, the Holy Spirit, through Harvest Ministries, has done so much to push our nation forward in a relevant, real and up-to-date way. Their ministry inspired me to outreach in the power of the Holy Spirit, combined with love. I have been teaching others the same principle. Many thousands are being touched by God through this growing international team of seed sowers.

Psychology in the Cafe

We held an event in our church and ran a series of workshops teaching psychology to Pre-Christians. People generally like and are attracted to psychology as a subject, and so we hoped to get a big crowd of attendees. I didn't necessarily want to teach psychology to facilitate an encounter with Jesus, but this was the best vehicle I had for attracting Pre-Christians to a workshop in a church building. The condition was that Christians could attend the workshops if they brought a Pre-Christian with them. The whole purpose of the workshop was to share Biblical truths using psychology-based models, linking psychological models with the Bible, to reflect Jesus, and draw folk into faith and the Kingdom. Mix in a few words of knowledge, the power of the Spirit, praying over each chair, and we have a powerful concoction for spreading Kingdom good news.

One or two Christians said, 'I'd like to come, but I don't know any non-Christians.' Jesus hung out with outcasts, including tax collectors and women previously involved in the sex industry. Let's join clubs and mingle with Pre-Christians.

One day I sensed Jesus saying to me;

'Find trouble, because where trouble is, I am.'

Can we teach on Matthew 28:18-20, and omit the word 'go'? Too often, we issue invitations to come and omit the command to go! *In the going, we find power.*

Pre-Christians Are Everywhere

You know, we are the only people on this planet with a legitimate and safe gift for healing people through the authority of Jesus' power and name. Yet, our health service is bursting at the seams, barely able to cope with the sick. We have the solution!

We must step out. Your neighbour has a headache? Step out. The postman has a toothache. Step out. Your delivery driver has a backache. Step out. I have heard countless stories of people stepping out to pray for healing and seeing conditions improve. It's just too easy an opportunity to miss.

And it's not even about the courage. It's about life or death for those who don't know Jesus. Step out. So, you look foolish looking like love? Step out. Step out. Step out.

You don't know what to say or give? 'Can I pray for you?' works. Then bless them.

The Humiliation of Rejection is Not Yours – Don't Fear It

One day I was working with a small crew of Jesus lovers out on the street. My friend was playing the guitar and singing, and I was handing out tracts and offering to pray for people. On that particular day, a lady passed by, hunched over a Sainsburys trolley and moving step by slow step. In the trolley was an oxygen cylinder, tubes from which ran into her nostrils. The shopping in her trolley looked weighty, and my heart went out to this resilient, determined, and obviously unwell woman.

It would be easy for me to get my car and offer her a lift home, and so I offered to help, but she declined and shuffled away. Around 30 minutes later, I spotted her in the town centre, less than 200 meters from where I had originally seen her. The town was packed with Saturday shoppers. She was sitting on a wall hunched over her trolley, breathing in gasps. Her lips were blue. My heart went out to her, and, thinking that her situation was physically worse than when I last offered help, I asked again if I could help her in any way, or offer a lift home?

This seemed to bring a miraculous and instantaneous healing, because she looked up and, filling her lungs, she bellowed full volume in the middle of the Saturday crowds, *'For God's sake!'*

Inwardly, I hoped this was a good start, after all, I was doing this for God's sake.

'It's people like you who make my life a misery!' she screamed, full lunged.

Now that was hardly fair, I thought, sensing the sideways looks from the Saturday shoppers.

'I don't want your bloody help!' The woman finally spat.

Hmm. That didn't go well. And I slunk away sheepishly into the crowd of shoppers, wryly smiling and puzzled. This was the most extreme 'no' I had ever received on the street, but it was still worth it, just to be true to myself. We can look like love, but love won't always be received well.

I don't know who said it, but one of the wisest sayings is that 'hurting people, hurt people.' I did it for Jesus, and that is what mattered. He already took my rejection on the Cross and it stays with Him. We forgive and move on. It's not possible for you to be rejected. In rejecting you, He is rejected.

Healing on the Streets

Healing on the Streets is a wonderful method of reaching out to Pre-Christians and practicing healing ministry. Check out www.healingonthestreets.com for more information.

I went out with a wonderful crew of Christians from several churches, we offered to pray for healing out on Chelmsford's streets. It's a great ministry for learning how to pray for the sick, the boldness to outreach, unity with other Christians and being Kingdom in the community around you.

From all of the fantastic stories from my time with the team, one is foremost in my heart. A man wheeled himself past me in a wheelchair. He was around 60 years old, carrying shopping on the back of his chair.

'Excuse me, Sir,' I said. 'We are praying for people on the streets today. Would you be willing for us to pray a blessing on your life? It won't take 5 minutes, and you'll never see me again.'

The man raised his eyebrows and with a shrug of his shoulders, said, 'Yes, why not.' Perfect!

Reader, please understand that when I invited this man over for prayer, it was purely with the intention to bless his life. But God had another plan.

He was living in a nursing home after he developed a degenerative muscular disease and was rapidly losing mobility. He was only 65. I joined up with Dave, one of the team leaders, to pray, as we always pray in twos. We knelt down by the man whose name I cannot recall. I prayed my best prayer of blessing over him and waited for Dave to do the same before sending the guy off in his wheelchair. I stayed on my knees with my head bowed (I should have been watching!)

Then Dave prayed for the man's legs to be healed in the name of Jesus.

Give Love A-Way

I cringed. *No, Dave, no!' He is in a wheelchair. You can't pray for his legs to be healed!*

Dave carefully placed his hand on the man's legs (with permission) and said,

'In the name of Jesus, legs be strengthened. Test out your legs. Try standing up.'

I squeezed my eyes tightly shut and immediately determined never to pray with Dave again. He really had gone too far. Then I heard a creak and opened my eyes. The man, leaning on the side bars, was shifting himself slowly out of the wheelchair. He stood up, laughed, then he walked, and laughed some more. He actually started running around the Chelmsford Market Square, punching the air, laughing and shouting, 'I'm getting younger!'

God had healed him. I don't remember much more than that, other than my amazement and wonder that the man had been healed to run.

Signs point to the reality of God, and are meant to make people wonder.

To my embarrassment (I must forgive myself!), when he came back, I pushed his empty wheelchair toward him, expecting him to get back in. My feeble faith was struggling to believe. It still hadn't registered that he was healed to walk.

'No, it's okay.' He said, looking at me curiously. 'I prefer to push the wheelchair.' He walked away tall and strong, pushing the wheelchair, still laughing.

My friend Clive always says, particularly in the moments I feel most vulnerable, *'Just turn up. God will do the rest.'*

How true that is.

Find a Point of Agreement Rather Than a Point of Argument

There is much to agree on. It's so easy to fight for a position we don't need to fight for. In my opinion, apologetics are what we have left when we use arguments to persuade and ignore the power of signs and wonders. We can agree with much of what people say, if we are ready to listen and not defend. I discovered this through relying on the Holy Spirit for replies whenever I have no answer.

> **'Choosing to look like love will always supply the answer.'** *Word of Wisdom*

It's not unusual for Christians from other churches to try and convert me. I'm often a little sad to be preached at by another Christian who is keen to expound their theology and judge me for mine. I *was* that person until the conviction of God corrected me. The Lord spoke to me very clearly after a teaching session I had participated in. As I listened to the teaching from (remarkably?!) the same Bible as mine, I became more and more angry and resolved never to revisit that series of teaching sessions.

Afterwards, God said to me loudly and clearly: 'How dare you judge your brother for his theology when your brother doesn't judge you?'

Can we lay down our judgements of one another and choose to look like love and unconditional positive regard?

Managing 'Hot Potato' Topics

A woman angrily dismissed my question; 'Do you believe in God?' and replied, 'No, I believe in Darwin.'

I heard the point of agreement come out from my mouth as I said; 'That's great. God believed in Darwin, too.' After all, He created Darwin! Whether we believe that evolution created the animal kingdom, or whether or not the big bang theory explains the earth and its creation, we can always come back to Jesus.

Ultimately, I wasn't there at creation. It's my view that Genesis is a literal description of creation. I don't know where dinosaur bones came from, but this doesn't suggest to me that Jesus didn't tell the truth or that His death is not the most significant death in the whole of eternity. I simply don't know how dinosaurs fit into Genesis. Still, I'm not trying to win a position.

To look like love is the best we have.

A common concern is: if God is real, why doesn't He end suffering? Again, I bring Jesus in here. There is so much I don't know, but I do believe that Jesus came to the earth and experienced suffering on our behalf. We killed Him, through our greed, selfishness and destructive action, but He couldn't be held by death. He rose from the dead and offers us forgiveness, peace and healing from wounds.

God hates suffering, too. Why do 'good' people die? I don't know. One day, we will see clearly.

What about other religions? Again, I have to say the Cross is a pivotal point in history for all mankind, and Jesus died for everyone. This doesn't mean I believe everyone will reach Heaven, but we will eventually be judged by the condition of our heart. Will every Christian be accepted by Jesus? I have no idea. For some Christians, this lack of certainty is tantamount to heresy. I am happy not to know who will or won't be saved. Does everyone deserve a personal introduction to Jesus? I believe so. Father is quite capable of revealing His Son (in dreams, for example) without human intervention.

> *'"Not everyone who says to me, 'Lord, Lord,' will enter the kingdom of Heaven, but only the one who does the will of my Father who is in Heaven. Many will say to me on that day, 'Lord, Lord, did we not prophesy in your name and in your name drive out demons and, in your name, perform many miracles?' Then I will tell them plainly, 'I never knew you. Away from me, you evildoers!'"' Matthew 7:21-23*

We don't need all the answers to be able to share Jesus. Even Paul became all things to all men so that some might be saved.

> *'To the weak I became weak, to win the weak.' 1 Corinthians 9:22*

Does it mean that we ignore the gospel and water down our message to attract people into the Kingdom rather than convict them? No. The gospel looks like love.

'Love is the best attractor for Pre-Christians to a God who is Himself Love.' *Word of Wisdom*

We won't know all the answers. We don't need to. We need only point people to the One who really knows, and He is the Lord.

The gifts are easy; love is the challenge.

Avoid Christian Words That People May Not Understand

Christianese isn't an easy language for Pre-Christians to navigate! It's our native language, but a foreign language to the unchurched.

For example, in outreach, we try to avoid using the terms 'God' and 'Lord.' So many people have views of God that aren't biblically-based, like God being some vast impersonal cosmic force in the sky.

The term 'Lord' comes through revelation and relationship that Pre-Christians rarely have. **Jesus** is the simplest, most effective name to use when witnessing to others. After all, He is the way the truth and the life.

We point people in the direction of Jesus, because Jesus is the destination everyone must find.

Try to avoid the word sin, too. People don't understand it, and it can carry religious connotations of stereotypical Old Testament preachers calling people to repentance. The Holy Spirit brings conviction. The passion behind our beliefs doesn't not convict people. Describing sin as 'selfishness' makes the concept of sin accessible and understandable to Pre-Christians. Putting Self first, others second, and God last—the complete opposite of the order identified in the Greatest Commandment (Matthew 22:36-40)—this is sin.

Interestingly, when talking to New Agers or spiritualists, I may begin by talking to them about the Holy Spirit. Spiritualists and New Agers are often seeking a spiritual reality that they may not expect to exist in Christianity. They may not be aware of the risks and dangers involved in dealing with any spirit who is not Holy Spirit, the one who never deceives. He is the only safe Spirit. I explain this so that, with this knowledge, people have the choice as to whom or what they follow. We can't bludgeon people into the Kingdom based on their behaviour being right or wrong.

'To look like love is to look like God.' *Word of Wisdom*

Point People to Jesus

The foundational position for talking about Jesus is found in C.S. Lewis' treasured and helpful quote from Mere Christianity[7]. Lewis says Jesus isn't just some great moral teacher. He is what He claimed to be: God. If He isn't God, then He is a madman or a liar. Or He is telling the truth.

This is a quote I often use with people. I encourage them to read a gospel to discover who Jesus was, and what He did and said. It's important that people find out who Jesus is for themselves. I also find carrying a Gospel of Luke in my bag to be a handy tool.

It's the ultimate decision for every human being on this planet. If Jesus was telling the truth, then we should at least attempt to discover what He said. Pointing to Jesus is the best seed we can sow. Whatever the objection, conversation, attack, argument or question; we must get across the truth of a God who loved the world so much that He gave His only Son for us. A God who cared enough about our suffering to experience the ultimate in pain.

Always try to talk about Jesus to Pre-Christians.

Answering the Question 'Why?'

There is one question as common to the human condition as being born or dying. It's a universal question, one we all encounter, some of us many times. It is also the one question we rarely, if ever, get an answer to.

'Why?' is the one question we all have in common.

The question 'why?' is often born from pain. It carries a range of powerful emotions – vulnerability, anger, sadness, rage and suffering. It is often directed at God, questioning His goodness, love and/or power.

---

[7] *Mere Christianity, London: Collins, 1952*

If God really exists, why did He allow this?
Why is He mean, vindictive or uncaring?
Why doesn't He love me?
What did I do wrong?
Why didn't He stop it from happening?
Why call Himself good and loving if He doesn't stop bad things from happening to innocent people?

There is no easy answer. Neither should there be, in the face of humanity's pain, often the pain of someone in front of you, a friend, neighbour, family or stranger.

When I am asked 'Why?' by someone hurting, angry or genuinely perplexed, I keep love switched on and have to say, 'I don't know.' There is no clever response.

I might say that Jesus died asking the same question of His own Dad. A Dad He trusted and loved; a Dad He knew could rescue Him, who ultimately allowed Him to die a horrific death for you and for me. In Matthew 27:46 and Mark 15:34, Jesus asks: "My God, My God, why have you forsaken me?"

It was a question He didn't have answered this side of death. 'Dad, why did you forsake me? Why did you let this happen?' Yet, trust carried him over and kept the relationship intact. Trust that, in the face of abject cruelty and evil, where we (mankind) killed Him through thoughtless, selfish, corrupted actions, Jesus did not judge God as incompetent, powerless, heartless, ignorant, bad, or non-existent.

So, when people ask me the question 'why?' or suggest that God is somehow cruel or unloving, I remind them that Jesus asked the same question, and yet trusted a loving Father.

We can't explain someone else's pain away, but we can point them to Jesus who ultimately understands. The world needs to know that Jesus asked 'why?', too.

Don't Try to Convert People

We should never try to convert or put pressure on anyone to acknowledge Jesus. Converting a person is in fact an impossibility. We can lead them to Jesus, but it is always their choice to have a relationship with Him. Mostly, we sow seeds.

We are responsible for loving the neighbour in front of us but not for outcomes. The motivation for sowing seed must always be love. Judgement often smells of superiority, when we are dealing with people who aren't necessarily wilful and unbelieving. They are, in the main part, unaware of a Jesus who died for them personally. They are blind to the benefits of forgiveness and peace, unless we tell them.

At Harvest School, Heidi Baker taught us to love the one in front of us, and to 'go low and go slow.' To look like love.

I met a Christian woman on the street a few weeks back. She was angry about many things, and also expressed hatred in her views about many types of people, including me. Looking like love was the best I could give this woman. Jesus loved the lost. He had time for them. He healed them; He loved them.

> *He sent them away restored; love.*
> *He spent time with them; love.*
> *He provided for them; love.*
> *He cared; love.*

The majority of His rebukes were for the religious people who put the Law and the 'thou shalts' before love.

Let's be known by our fruit, the fruit of the Spirit.

We can be at our least loving when we try to 'do' evangelism i.e. push Jesus into another's life. We also need to be careful of the tracts we hand out, avoiding tracts with religious language or heavy in condemnation and coercion. Can we look like love? Love points to a loving God and is more challenging than being judgmental.

Were you won by His love or coerced by fear? Let's go and do likewise.

It will be an incredible joy to see Heaven populated with people whose lives we have touched with love.

Is this your goal?

The Principle of Giving

We see a wonderful principle in the Bible, many times, where there is more power in giving (more blessed to give than receive - Acts 20:35). And we receive multiplication in return for our giving. It's beautiful when we give simply for its own sake; for the pure joy of giving love A-Way.

> *"Truly I tell you," Jesus said to them, "no one who has left home or wife or brothers or sisters or parents or children for the sake of the kingdom of God will fail to receive many times as much in this age, and in the age to come eternal life." Luke 18:29 - 30*

Jesus was so clever and wise when he told us not to pray for the harvest, but for workers to be sent out. Feeling unequipped or ungifted can result in hesitation to get involved, but those are not enough reasons to avoid participating in reaching out to Pre-Christians. Sometimes, we just need a method.

I recognised that offering something when approaching folk on the street provides a half-way house to buffer that helpless feeling. If I have something to give away, I am less likely to experience rejection!

I encourage our congregation to bring items like chocolates or flowers to give away at the Free Family Fun Festival and other special events in town. The red rose—a love symbol—wrapped in tissue is often a perfect gift. Even a cheesy (but true statement) delivered at this time is possible.

'Have a rose/flower. God loves you.' (Carnations work, too!)

If you're brave, you might add something like:

'May I pray a blessing on your life?' Or, *'Is there anything I can pray about for you today?'*

Having a one liner that you feel comfortable with works best. I tend to say, 'Excuse me, you will probably never see me again, so can I ask you a question?'

Mostly, the answer is yes.

Then I follow up with something like; 'Do you have any spiritual beliefs?' 'Do you pray?' 'Do you believe in God?'

Using the chalkboard with its menu of Holy Spirit-inspired ministry opportunities is always the best means for me to talk with folk, but having a starting point works, too.

My encouraging Christians to give away chocolates and flowers, with no motive other than to look like love, deeply annoyed one of our church members. They sent an angry email, suggesting that offering flowers and chocolates to passers-by was like 'sticking plasters on lepers.'

Offering flowers or chocolates will never create disciples, but they are good opportunities to connect and, hopefully, start a conversation. Giving something away equips people with a conversation starter.

The ideal is that everyone feels able and equipped to deliberately reach out and share Jesus with their neighbour. This is why Jesus told us to pray for workers to go out into the harvest field. The fields really are ripe.

What Can You Give A-Way?

I heard the great story of a church in England who wanted to outreach to their community. They thought about all the things that they were good at and what they might possibly give away, and concluded that they were great at hugs. A hug was their thing. And so, one Saturday, the good folk from this church went to their local town for a few hours, requesting permission to offer hugs. They were brave in giving their love A-Way.

Their allotted time concluded, one of the church leaders stopped in a shop to buy something on his way home. He stood patiently in a queue behind a woman.

'What's been happening in town today?' The woman asked the cashier when she reached the counter 'I saw people hugging one another, laughing and smiling! It feels like the whole atmosphere in the town has changed.'

'Ah,' replied the storekeeper. 'Those were Christians from the local church. They were giving away free hugs today.'

The lady being served looked perplexed. 'That can't have been Christians.' she said. 'Christians always look so miserable, and the people I saw were all smiling and happy.'

Do What You Can

One of the loveliest, most touching pieces of outreach I have encountered was initiated by a couple from my church. Normally, the concept of evangelism might make them lock their doors and hide. However, the wife wrote out Bible verses on scrolls of paper and carefully placed them in a box. They came to the Free Fun Family Festival in Colchester, and held out the box for people to take a hand written scroll, trusting that God would speak to the person through the Bible verse. The principle of giving, expecting nothing back, is immensely loving. They gave what they could, and what they gave was so quietly powerful. They prayed for several people that day, and, no doubt, also prayed that everyone receiving a Bible verse would be blessed.

'We don't need professional evangelists; we simply need willing lovers.' *Word of Wisdom*

Evangelism Looks Like Love

We run an event in Kingsland called Free Family February Fun day. On what we believed to be the greyest and most miserable Saturday of the year, we invited the community to the building to participate in free games and activities with concerts from local musicians. Around a thousand people showed up. Our Spiritual Café team was kept busy all day, ministering to Pre-Christians in prophetic words, prayer, healing prayer, etc.

With the volume of people coming through, the café serving drinks and food was heaving all day. At one point, I popped into the kitchen for a coffee, and spotted Roger, one of our congregation, bent over the full sink, washing up with sweat running down his brow in the hot and hectic kitchen. The team clearing up brought him dirty cups, mugs, plates and cutlery and Roger, uncomplaining, scrubbed for hours. A hidden hero.

All day long, the team and I worked hard ministering to our guests. We didn't have enough people to keep up with demand, and we had specifically asked Christians not to come in for a session because Sunday is reserved for Christians to receive prayer and prophetic input. Everyone receiving ministry was Pre-Christian, and some gave their lives after an encounter with Jesus.

I was disappointed by the few people willing to work in the Spiritual Café, struggling to understand why gifted people might not offer to support this outreach. But then the conviction (God's wisdom) hit me that everything we were doing that day was outreach. Every action communicated love for Jesus' sake.

Roger, slaving over a hot sink, served his heart out for Jesus. Without Roger, the café wouldn't have worked. People would have become disillusioned by the mess and lack of supply, and not enjoyed a good time, or even ministry, without Roger in the kitchen.

So often, high profile ministry gets the glory whilst the behind-the-scenes ministry (playgroups, welcome team, soup run, games night, children's ministry etc) can have their powerful impact overlooked.

We are a body. We work in unity.

At the end of the day, knowing their disappointment about the lack of workers in the Spiritual Café, I said to my team, *'Isn't it sad that we are the only ones focused on outreach?'*

Nods and frowns.

'But actually, do you know who worked hardest today to outreach to the community?' Shaking of heads as they looked at each other.

'Roger,' I continued. 'I saw him sweating for hours at the sink, washing up. At lunchtime he sat, exhausted, eating a sandwich, before returning to the sink. That man worked tirelessly today to reach out to others.'

I had learned my lesson.

Let's celebrate the hidden heroes and share the public victories.

> *'So whether you eat or drink or whatever you do, do it all for the glory of God.'* 1 Corinthians 10:31

Treat People Like They Matter

We come into contact with people every day, everywhere. We are guaranteed to meet people. How often do we care more about them than we care about our agenda? How important is the cashier? Care about their day. When you go out, be intentional around those you meet.

You may be the only Jesus that people get to meet.

Please, look at people as you go about. Make them matter. Look like love. We have this one opportunity in a lifetime to make a difference. Be more concerned about the other than you are about yourself.

Manage Your Metre

When someone initiates a conversation e.g. asks a question, makes a comment or chats, know there may be a reason. It's my theory, as you know, that if someone steps into my world, no matter how innocuous the encounter may be, God has probably sent them. I watch and I listen. It's a divine appointment.

We are people of purpose; let's live with intention.

Give Love A-Way

Neil Loxley, the leader of Kingsland Church, owns a motorbike, and seizes the opportunity to ride it. On this occasion, he invited me to ride pillion to attend a training session in Central London. It made sense to go by motorbike and my adventurous nature was kindled! As we crossed London Bridge, lost and in search of parking, we didn't foresee the engine catching fire. The motorbike stalled mid traffic and smoke wafted from the engine.

As I slid off the seat to escape the smoke, my leg got stuck. I wobbled into the road in the middle of London Bridge, and lay sprawled in a bus lane to gasps from the passing crowd!

I'm probably incredibly annoying in my belief that Romans 8:28 holds good in EVERY situation. '*All things* work for the good...' Not some things, nor most things, but *all* things. *Everything.*

Neil wasn't impressed with my joy filled-belief, as his beloved motorbike smoked, immobile on the London Bridge pavement. Incidentally, this was just weeks before the terror attacks on the same bridge. We prayed the bike would remain secure and without a parking ticket till our return. Highly unlikely, in the natural. Leaving a post-it note on the bike on a windy day probably wasn't great thinking either. However, we were at least parked in central London, so, leaving the bike to the mercy of Heaven, we ran to the training venue, me in my oversized, borrowed bike leathers.

The AA arranged to collect the bike after our course ended. When we got back, we rejoiced that:

- A) The bike was still parked on London bridge.
- B) It had no ticket, even though the post-it note had blown away!

The very nice AA man loaded the bike onto the back of the truck.

'There's a reason why this happened.' I said to Neil. 'I'm sure of it.'

Unfortunately, Neil didn't see the burning of his bike as a fortuitous act of God. He wasn't perky and prepared like me, when the AA driver placed us in the front of the cab for the 1.5-hour journey back to Colchester in rush hour traffic. The driver had unexpectedly entered our space! There had to be a reason.

I worked so hard to get a conversation going with the driver, relying on the Spirit to open up the conversation. It turned out he had Jewish parentage and an interest in spiritual things. We talked about Jesus, answered his questions and had a deep and meaningful conversation for a long stretch of the journey. He dropped us off in Colchester, allowed us to pray with him before he left, and was touched in a powerful way by the Holy Spirit as we prayed for him. Romans 8:28 prevailed and we treated this driver like he mattered to Heaven, which he did. A divine set up, I'm sure. A seed sewn.

We must live as though we are meant to be in this place, at this time, for a reason.

Let's live with an intentional mindset. 'Who do you want to bless today, Lord?'

My friend Alison had often listened to me talking about 'managing your meter.' She decided to put this mindset in place when she travelled to Heathrow airport to catch a flight out. The airport was busy and the café packed, and a woman made her way to Alison's table and asked if she could sit. Alison didn't mind, and the woman sat down. As idle chit chat followed about holidays and destinations, Alison noticed a bandage on the woman's wrist. Because the woman had entered into her space, she asked what the problem was, stepped out in faith, risking rejection or embarrassment, and asked if she could pray for the wrist.

'Jesus heals today.' Alison told the woman who agreed to be prayed for.

The woman told Alison she was heading to Washington, as she held a senior position in the United Nations, and was touched by Jesus in a profound way.

We never know who we might be praying for!

'Can I Pray for You?'

Five of the most powerful words you can ever use. When your neighbour tells you, they are having a bad day. When the delivery driver drops off a parcel. When you're at the checkout or the corner shop. When you're waiting for a bus. At the hairdresser. With your family, friends. At work. Walking the dog. At the gym. On the train.

Five powerful words you can offer – **'Can I pray for you?'**

> *'"We have been made a spectacle to the whole universe, to angels as well as to human beings. We are fools for Christ, but you are so wise in Christ! We are weak, but you are strong! You are honoured, we are dishonoured!"' 1 Corinthians 4:9-10*

If you are full of the Holy Spirit, He will use you to witness to the life and reality of Jesus. If you aren't already full, be filled. He makes us witnesses for Jesus. Don't **do** boldness. Through the Holy Spirit, **become** boldness! Choose to step out.

Our stepping out in faith is the 'going and the sending' we are commanded to fulfil.

When you pray for someone, tell them you will only take two minutes, they can keep their eyes open if they wish, and ask to lay a hand on their shoulder. We do this because there is power in the laying on of hands. The Holy Spirit in you will connect with the person who has your hand on them. During the COVID-19 period, we are finding it equally powerful to ask the person to lay a hand on their own heart. Since you believe God will be at work, step out in faith and say,

'You will experience God's touch. You may feel hot, warm, or peaceful. It won't be bad or scary, because Jesus is love.' Then pray your best, simple prayer.

'Jesus, thank you for (name of person). Thank you for their life. I know you love (name of person) and so, I ask that you touch (name of person's) life.'

Then, leave a silence for God to work. You could command the sickness specifically to leave. e.g. 'Pain go, in Jesus Name.'

If you feel it's right, don't wait. Just do it.

Ask 'Can I pray for you?'

Then say 'Thank you'!

Here is a story from my friend Jenny who simply said; 'Can I pray for you?'

> "I had to leave a pair of boots with a shoe mender and found a suitable place to leave them for repair within a local large supermarket.

It was somewhat busy when I returned to collect my boots from the designated area, and I had time to notice that the man behind the counter had a plaster on his left hand, and was having considerable difficulty lifting customers' shoes with that hand. I overheard him tell the customer ahead of me that he had damaged his index finger badly and the doctors had said it may not return to full strength and usage. As I waited, I reflected that these statements were not what I believed. God can heal index fingers—they are not impossible to Him. I was conscious of the queue and started to pray that nobody would join in behind me so that I could offer to pray for this man's finger.

Nobody joined, so I went forward and requested the repair I had come for, as well as asking some questions about why he had a plaster on his hand. During this transaction a man arrived behind me awaiting service but I was convinced that I had to pray for healing.

As he handed me the receipt for my shoe repairs, feeling a little stupid, I said, "I believe God can heal fingers. Would it be ok if I prayed for yours?"

He agreed.

Sheepishly and well aware of the man behind me, I said, "Finger be healed and completely restored in Jesus' name."

I made a quick getaway after that, not looking back before exiting the store! Two weeks later, I returned to collect my repaired boots. I was surprised to see that the bandage was no longer on the man's hand and that he was working quite normally.

When I approached his counter, he recognised me and started to tell me that he had full recovery of his finger. He went on to say he was a climber and that he could demonstrate to the surgeon looking after him that he could use the finger to pull himself up when climbing.

I said God had performed the miracle, paid for my boots and left.

Some months later I returned for a different reason. Again, he recognised me! I asked him how his hand was doing and he had no problem with it. He then went on to say he had taken his son climbing during a recent school holiday and the weather turned out to be less than ideal. He was worried about continuing the climb as he felt responsible for his son, so he stopped and waited. As he did this, he saw a rainbow and decided then and there that it was okay to proceed to the top. It was indeed okay and both father and son had a brilliant day.

On hearing this tale my comment to him was that he had heard God speak to him, as God's rainbow was a promise.

I have no idea whether this man has a faith or no faith but I learned that I have to be bold and pray for people."

We sow the seeds. God grows them.

When People Aren't Healed Immediately

Jesus told us we would do greater things than He did because He was going to the Father. His physical departure allowed for His Spiritual entrance through the Holy Spirit.

Praying healing prayers for Pre-Christians can sometimes be easier than praying for Christians. I have seen many Pre-Christians healed, and prayed for as many who have not appeared to receive healing. When praying for healing for a Christian, I always give them the freedom from responsibility for being healed.

'It's not your responsibility to be healed,' I tell them. 'It's God's responsibility to heal.'

This saves on the guilt trip some people experience if they are not aware of any change after prayer.

Is it somehow my fault? They wonder.

There is so much we don't know, but carrying guilt or condemnation if we have not yet experienced healing is unhelpful. 'Yet' being the operative word, here.

Keep asking, keep believing. Don't get swallowed up in bitterness or shame.

Why people aren't always instantaneously healed is a big question, especially in the light of the New Testament where Jesus heals everyone who comes to Him, as do the apostles, in the Book of Acts.

Our questions must drive us toward God, and not away from Him.

We also shouldn't assume there hasn't been an answer, if there's no obvious immediate outcome. The Word of God holds good and true. Jesus says:

> *'"Ask and it will be given to you; seek and you will find; knock and the door will be opened to you."' Matthew 7:7*

It can be the hardest thing to step out with faith, pray for healing, and not see the person healed immediately. Encouraging and reassuring people that God is a God of love, and that there is no sickness in Heaven is important. It may be a weak method of preparing to deal with this outcome, but I often say to people:

'I know Jesus still heals today. I have prayed for many people and they have been immediately healed, and prayed for many others but not seen an instant change. Sometimes, healing happens over time. God is loving and powerful, even when we don't see an instant response. Is it ok to pray for you?'

When using the spiritual gifts, keep love in sight.

Establish the Person's Name and Make Eye Contact

People who don't listen don't tend to give eye contact. If someone turns away when you are speaking or you focus elsewhere when others are speaking to you, the reality is that we have stopped listening. Eye contact is one of our most powerful outreach tools.

> *'"The eye is the lamp of the body. If your eyes are healthy, your whole body will be full of light. But if your eyes are unhealthy, your whole body will be full of darkness. If then the light within you is darkness, how great is that darkness!"' Matthew 6:22-24*

When I am intentional in my lifestyle, living like people matter; when I am ready to be the divine appointment someone may need, I give eye contact. It's simple. Passing through the checkout, I look at the cashier. In the eyes. Does she or he seem tired, or sad, or happy, or helpful, or angry? How does she or he look? I am intentional. What we see will determine what someone might need.

Can I find something good to say?

'How is your day going?'
'What are you looking forward to doing after work?'
'Do you have a dream for your life?'
'If you won an all-expenses paid holiday, where would you go if money was no object?'

Lift up their heads from the mundane. Be extraordinary.

Can you be more interested in the person you encounter than the task you need to complete?
Stay switched on to love. Make that choice. Many of us lack a ministry outlet for weeks, sometimes even years. When life feels this way, we need to ask ourselves whether or not we have switched off to living with Jesus. The harvest is so plentiful and the workers so few. Can we choose to look like love every day, even in the car park?

It's a sobering thought that, if each Christian brought just one person to Jesus just once a year, the church would double in one year and experience exponential future growth.

We must live like people matter.

What Is God's Will for My Life?

If we are waiting for direction, today holds as many ministry opportunities as we choose to be awake to. Our commission and ministry are clear in Matthew 22:35–40, Mark 12:28–34 and Luke 10:27.

> *'One of them, an expert in the law, tested him with this question: "Teacher, which is the greatest commandment in the Law?" Jesus replied: "'Love the Lord your God with all your heart and with all your soul and with all your mind.' This is the first and greatest commandment. And the second is like it: 'Love your neighbour as yourself.' All the Law and the Prophets hang on these two commandments."' Matthew 22:35-40*

The two greatest commandments hold good for everyday life, and we can practice them daily. Love is our ministry, wherever we are. Let's not wait for tomorrow. Don't switch off. Stay switched on.

Living is about His will; not mine.

Everyday Outreach

We have seen that outreach doesn't have to happen someplace special. An old guy called Roy got saved by Jesus late in life. After he retired, he would head in to Colchester town, sit on a wall, and hand out tracts to passers-by. He became well known as, rain, shine or snow, Roy Makin took his place on the same wall, every day except for Sunday.

'I used to be a grumpy old bus driver.' He would tell anyone who took a tract from his extended hand, 'but then I found the Lord'. Day after day, Roy was faithful. He handed out scores of tracts and often led several people to a commitment to Jesus during the course of a day. Phenomenal.

A few years before he died, he had a heart attack outside on his way into town, and recounted being dead for about fifteen minutes before being revived by paramedics.

After recuperating in hospital, he headed back into town. Then, he developed an ulcer on his leg that didn't seem to heal. Roy continued going into town. The wound became gangrenous and his leg was eventually amputated. He couldn't wait to recover from this, so he obtained a mobility scooter and headed back in to town by scooter and bus. The man was phenomenal or, possibly, just gloriously saved.

When Roy died, I determined to honour his space on the wall. So did several other Christians. It can be a task I don't look forward to each week, but I love it after we finish and have had a good time. Week after week, we train others to use their spiritual gifts with Pre-Christians, head to Colchester town centre and present ourselves as living sacrifices to God; the fragrance of life.

Was there ever a time in your life when you needed to know the reality of God? Have you been through 'the valley of the shadow of death' (Psalm 23), or a time of darkness when only God could rescue the situation? That's my motivation for going.

'When we know love, we can give love.' *Word of Wisdom*

In Matthew 28:19, Jesus said, 'Go', not 'wait for them to come'. Not invite them to our buildings. He said to 'Go.' Where can you go? If we all go, the world will soon be transformed by His Presence. Your reaching out matters. When you go to the hairdresser, school, workplace, recycling centre and use these tools and principles, you will stop preparing for outreach and become outreach. The flow of the river.

You Are Kingdom in Your Workplace

> *'And whatever you do, whether in word or deed, do it all in the name of the Lord Jesus, giving thanks to God the Father through him.' Colossians 3:17*

You don't have to go to Africa to be a missionary. There is no second class calling when it comes to mission. Our mission is to love our neighbour and be salt and light. Mission will always be where you are. If you earn a daily living, then your calling to trust is no different than a person living abroad for the sake of mission. Pray for your work colleagues, pray for the business, pray over each chair.

'Mission is a mindset, and not a place.' *Word of Wisdom*

Are we ready to say; 'Can I pray for you?' Check out Heaven in Healthcare on the Eastgate Church website (www.heaveninhealthcare.com). There are countless stories of professionals in the NHS who make a difference for the Kingdom by staying switched on to God through engaging with Heaven during work hours.

Be inspired to *be* the difference. Love your neighbour. Make coffee for your colleagues. Buy fruit. Cakes. Remember birthdays. Care about the weekend. Wash up. Look like love. Whatever it takes to be like Jesus.

You have His Presence. Everywhere you go, you carry change, because God is in you. Walk with intention. Know His power. Engage with love.

'The fruit of the Spirit communicates the truth of the gospel.' *Word of Wisdom*

When we are filled with the Spirit, we look like love, peace and joy. We are irritatingly above our circumstances; seated in Heavenly realms with Christ Jesus, and wise in our strategy for the issues each day brings. Above our circumstances and not below.

Do you look like love? Be filled with the Spirit. Do you look like joy? Be filled with the Spirit. Do you look like peace? Be filled with the Spirit. Do you look like patience, goodness, kindness, faithfulness, gentleness? Be filled with the Spirit.

Do you look like self-control? Father, fill us with the Spirit. Jesus, give us the Holy Spirit. Holy Spirit, fill us with you!

Did you ever wonder why a vast proportion of our culture appears to revolve around alcohol and drunkenness? My theory is that people are thirsty. They take a drink to feel better.

Once you have tasted of the Holy Spirit, your desire for the counterfeit (and its consequences) will never be the same. No one has ever had a hangover from being full of the Holy Spirit. Paul tells us to get drunk on the Spirit, not on wine. Let's find our rest, peace and joy in Jesus.

> *"'Come, all you who are thirsty, come to the waters;*
> *and you who have no money, come, buy and eat!*
> *Come, buy wine and milk without money and without cost.*
> *Why spend money on what is not bread, and your labour on*
> *what does not satisfy? Listen, listen to me, and eat what is*
> *good, and you will delight in the richest of fare.'"* Isaiah 55:1-2

'God Bless You'

Another simple way of making your faith transparent is to say, 'bless you' at the end of your long or brief meeting. 'Thanks, and God bless you' go together easily. When we mean the words 'bless you' and really believe they can change someone else's world, we will be more inclined to bless other people.

Talk with and listen to the Spirit of the Father, the Spirit of Jesus: The Holy Spirit.

CHAPTER 14 – HOW TO WALK IN THE SPIRIT

He is *your* Holy Spirit

When our head is in Heaven, we think like Jesus. When our heart is in Heaven, we love like Jesus. When our feet are led by Heaven, we are in step with the Holy Spirit.

So how do we walk in the Spirit? I'd like to outline seven steps learned from my journey to date:

1. Seek First His Kingdom and His Righteousness

> *"'So do not worry, saying, 'What shall we eat?' or 'What shall we drink?' or 'What shall we wear?' For the pagans run after all these things, and your Heavenly Father knows that you need them. But seek first his kingdom and his righteousness, and all these things will be given to you as well.'" Matthew 6:31 - 33*

On the one hand, much of life is spent chasing resource for living. Worries about resource are symptoms of orphan thinking. An orphan doesn't have a great big Parent looking out for his or her welfare. It can be hard to trust that 'the Lord will provide'.

It's easy to run after resource and model one's day around income and work. Kingdom becomes a lesser priority than making ends meet. We can unconsciously prioritise 'work' above Kingdom with thoughts like 'I don't have time to pray,' 'I'm too busy to read my Bible'. God fits into my tight schedule, instead of my schedule fitting in with Heaven's agenda.

Have you ever had such thoughts? We prioritise what is most important to us. Last thing at night, before we crawl into bed and sleep off our long and tiring day, we clean our teeth. Our teeth have an automatic appointment with the toothbrush because dental hygiene is our priority.

We should never squeeze God into our agenda and have Him bless our plans. We must seek out His will and purpose, and gift our lives to Him daily.

'Don't waste the dawn.' *Word of Wisdom*

Even if we are financially secure ('retired' in the world's terms but not retired from the Kingdom) or still working but wealthy, are we focused on satisfying ourselves and living to our own agenda, or living for Him? Where have we put our purpose?

Are we seeking His Kingdom first? This isn't about legalism and procedure, it's about the condition of the heart. Where is our focus?

Are we living in self-pursuits or the pursuit of God?

We have an audience of one. Can we truly say that we are stewarding our time by focusing first on His Kingdom? Paul tells us to fix our eyes and thoughts on Jesus. To adopt a position whereby our eyes focus vertically and not horizontally. Are we fixed on Heaven? Vertical vision is seeing the world from Heaven's agenda. Horizontal vision is being side tracked by others (family, friends, church, or work), or distracted as we pat ourselves up and down asking; 'Am I okay? What am I feeling?'

> **'Keep vertical vision.'** *Word of Wisdom*

Distraction is a brilliant tactic of the enemy. Too full of my life to be full of His life in me. Can we lay it all down?

Are we spiritually alive? Do we have our priorities right? Jesus identifies the stranger as our neighbour and commands us to love our neighbour as we love ourselves. Who is our priority? Are we focusing our time and resource on family? Spouse? Friends? Work? Career? Church? We must wake up to our priorities.

In the morning, ask the following questions: 'Lord, what is your agenda today? Who do you want me to encounter? Lord, direct my feet.'

Compartmentalisation is another name for control. Is God in our box? Is He a slot in our day? Our week? Our year? What does it mean for us to seek first His Kingdom and His righteousness? Surrender is a great place to start. If we think this world is a greater reality than the coming world, we may have it wrong.

> **'If we don't challenge our current habits, we won't get back our true power and His true Glory.'** *Word of Wisdom*

'If' can be a pivotal moment. What must you surrender to His safe keeping? When you seek His Kingdom and righteousness first, everything else will fall into place.

Everything. It just will.

2. *Know Your Place on This Planet*

Are we living like we don't belong on this planet? Or is the physical world more real to us than the unseen Kingdom? How do we know if we are more engaged with the world than we are in the Kingdom?

> *'So we fix our eyes not on what is seen, but on **what is
> unseen**, since what is seen is temporary, but what is
> unseen is eternal.' 2 Corinthians 4:18*

How do we fix our eyes on what is 'unseen'? We pray and read the Word. We surrender to a God who is alive, well, powerful, kind and loving. We believe. We keep faith.

The Old Testament pointed to a coming Kingdom; a metaphorical march towards a promised land flowing with milk and honey. We are still in pursuit of this Kingdom even though the Kingdom is within us now. There will be a time when we reach the Kingdom of Heaven and live the eternal life with the Lord.

> *'...Their mind is set on earthly things. But our
> citizenship is in Heaven. And we eagerly await a Saviour
> from there, the Lord Jesus Christ, who, by the
> power that enables him to bring everything under his
> control, will transform our lowly bodies so that they will
> be like his glorious body.' Philippians 3:20-21*

- ➢ 'Turn the other cheek.' Jesus said.
- ➢ 'Don't store up things for yourself on earth.' Jesus taught.
- ➢ 'Love your enemies.' He directs us.

Our lives are totally contrary to the things valued in the world. The great men and women of faith identified in Hebrews 11 often awaited the promise:

> *'All these died in faith, without receiving the promises, but having seen them and having welcomed them from a distance, and having confessed that they were strangers and exiles on the earth. For those who say such things make it clear that they are seeking a country of their own. And indeed if they had been thinking of that country from which they went out, they would have had opportunity to return.' Hebrews 11:13-16*

'We trust His resources in us when we cannot find our own. We surrender.' *Word of Wisdom*

Pleasures and peace are not our sole purpose for being. Pursuit of God is the way forward.

3. Practice Surrender

Can we say to the Lord, 'Here I am', and let our 'now' belong to Him? 'Here I am' is generally a response to someone calling us. We see five great heroes of faith in the Old Testament answering God's call and commission with this very response.

- Abraham said it in Genesis 22:1. This was in the context of Abraham being asked to sacrifice his beloved son Isaac to God. He surrendered.
- Jacob said it twice, in Genesis 31:11 and Genesis 46:2. Jacob struggles with God and overcomes. He surrenders His will.
- Moses said it in Exodus 3:4 when God called to him from the burning bush. He leads the Israelites out from the oppression of Egypt. He surrenders.
- Samuel said it in 1 Samuel 3:4. The Lord called to Samuel as a child when the voice of God had departed for many years from Israel.
- Isaiah said it in Isaiah 6:8. This is a response to a God who is asking; "Whom shall I send? And who will go for us?"

Surrendering to God isn't passive or weak. Surrender can involve great challenge and struggle as we wrestle and die to what, on occasions, seems counterintuitive.

> 'Then he called the crowd to him along with his disciples and said: "Whoever wants to be my disciple must deny themselves and take up their Cross and follow me. For whoever wants to save their life will lose it, but whoever loses their life for me and for the gospel will save it. What good is it for someone to gain the whole world, yet forfeit their soul?" Mark 8:34-36

There is an intentional choice to pick up and carry our cross. Dying to self isn't easy. Buddhists believe ego is the great obstacle to 'enlightenment', but Christians know the Cross is the point of rescue, redemption and turnaround. We must surrender our ego (or self) to Jesus in order to achieve true 'enlightenment' – oneness with Jesus through the Holy Spirit.

Our flesh is at war with our Heaven-focused needs and desires.

> 'Then he returned to his disciples and found them sleeping. "Couldn't you men keep watch with me for one hour?" he asked Peter. "Watch and pray so that you will not fall into temptation. The spirit is willing, but the flesh is weak." He went away a second time and prayed, "My Father, if it is not possible for this cup to be taken away unless I drink it, may your will be done." When he came back, he again found them sleeping, because their eyes were heavy.' Matthew 26:40 - 43

Practice power by waiting on the Presence of God. Find a physical place or position where you can go to surrender. Hands wide open, heart and mind willing, ears and eyes attentive to Presence, allowing Him to saturate, enliven and quicken you.

'Our everything for His everything.' *Word of Wisdom*

4. Live from Your True Identity

You will have already read the earlier Chapter on identity. One final point in relation to living like a reflection of Jesus:

We must be wary of the confession of our mouths. The spoken word contains power, which we see in Genesis 1 when God speaks creation into being. We are made in God's image, and yet we frequently speak in negative confessions.

> *'I'm no good at that.'*
> *'I can't do it.'*
> *'It's impossible.'*
> *'I'm so unlucky.'*
> *'I'm always overlooked.'*
> *'I eventually get rejected.'*
> *'I just can't break free.'*
> *'I'm sick and tired of this.'*
> *'It will never work.'*
> *'It's going to get worse with time.'*
> *'It's a ticking time-bomb.'*

Self-talk can be subtle and insidious, because speech overflows from the heart, thinking and beliefs.

Recently, as a young woman walked past me in town, her paper carrier bag inexplicably split open at the bottom, and a horoscope candle in a glass jar fell out and smashed.

'I'm so unlucky.' She said to me, stooping down to pick up the remnants. 'It's the story of my life.'

'Funny you should say that.' I replied. 'I just happen to be standing here, and your bag splits.' I pointed to the chalkboard with its ministry menu on it. 'Why don't we ask Jesus to give you the final word? What he says counts.'

She genuinely laughed, and we symbolically screwed up her useless bag and put it into a bin, and Jesus revealed words of knowledge through the Holy Spirit. These words could change her destiny. It was totally awesome – from a negative confession to the truth from Heaven.

'To saturate ourselves in His identity is to discover our real self.' *Word of Wisdom*

We can easily wear labels the world gives when God may have other plans for health or restoration. Our words can inadvertently reinforce such labels where our perfect identity from God looks like healing and restoration.

'As you speak, so it will be.' *Word of Wisdom*

One of the joys of the Spanish language is the quirkiness of the verb 'to have' in relation the English verb we commonly use, which is 'to be.'

Whereas we might ask: 'Are you cold?' In Spanish, we ask; *'tienes frio?'* which translates; 'Do you have cold?'

In English we would ask: 'Are you tired?' which implies a permanent state or identity. In Spanish it is; *'tienes cansada* (fem)?' Which translates as, 'Do you have tiredness?'

This is important, because the spoken word does not imply a permanent condition. 'I am tired.'

There are two verbs for 'To be' in Spanish: A permanent state of being is represented by the verb 'Ser'. 'I am Karen,' is a permanent state, covered by the verb 'Ser': 'Soy Karen.' A temporary state is reflected in the verb 'estar', implying a temporary state of being. For example, 'Are you unwell?' translates as 'estas mal?' 'Are you temporarily unwell?'

In a vivid and memorable dream, God once showed me that we can own symptoms when we feel unwell, which makes it difficult to shake them off. He explained that the symptoms themselves are not the problem as they can be very real. However, taking ownership through our language can create a permanent identity.

> 'I am short-sighted.'
> 'It's going to get worse with time.'
> 'I am seriously ill.'

Symptoms are not usually eradicated by positive thinking; and medicine and the medical profession are wonderful God-given tools and gifts to assist in healing. However, I learned from this dream not to allow my language to make the problem become my reality. 'I have the symptoms of a cold,' for example, as opposed to 'I have a cold.'

We can easily underestimate and misuse the self-declaration; 'I AM.'

Jesus' identity was consolidated and proclaimed by the Father after John baptised Jesus in the Jordan river:

> 'And a voice from Heaven said, "This is my
> Son, whom I love; with him I am well pleased."'
> Matthew 3:17, Mark 1:11, Luke 3:22.

Father made three points to affirm Jesus' identity:

1. You are my Son.
2. I love you.

3. *I am pleased with you.*

It is no different with you. At the point at which Jesus understood who He was; **I am Son**: He understood His position; **I am loved**: He understood His purpose; **I am pleased with you**: He began public ministry.

You are no different. You are Son, or Daughter. You are loved by Father. He is pleased with you. You don't have to do anything to make Him pleased. He already is.

Embrace and allow God's Spirit to transform who you are. There's no need to try and make Him pleased any longer. He already is.

5. Live Holy

In both the Old and New Testaments, we are called to be holy. Not *do*, but *be* holy.

> *'But just as he who called you is holy, so be holy in all you do; for it is written: "Be holy, because I am holy."'*
> 1 Peter 1:15-16

Will-power and choice won't do this for us. Only Holy Spirit in us can truly complete us.

Being 'holy' is not very fashionable. Holiness is a high standard to attain, unless we recognise that holy is something we become, and not something we do. The great paradox is that becoming often precedes doing.

What we surrender to Heaven is transformed by Heaven.

By His very nature, the Holy Spirit of the Father—the Spirit of Jesus—is holy. As with everything He touches, the light in Him becomes holiness and light in you. This is why we are in a journey of transformation, because the holiness Heaven sent in the form of God's Spirit is changing us into the likeness of Jesus.

> What are our eyes looking at?
> What are our ears listening to?
> What do we spend our time doing?
> What are our priorities?
> For whom are we living?

Can I be holy because He is holy? Can you align your heart, mind, soul and strength with Heaven through a surrendered self? Don't feel pressured; it's a journey. Use your words to surrender to Him.

'The rest will follow.' *Word of Wisdom*

6. Fellowship with The Holy Spirit

'Compartmentalising in our lives can lead to compartmentalising God.' *Word of Wisdom*

You have seen the key and pivotal message of this book at the end of each chapter:

'Talk with and listen to the Spirit of the Father, the Spirit of Jesus: The Holy Spirit.'

A church leader's wife, having struggled to connect with God for decades, began talking with the Holy Spirit. Her connection with God was transformed. This week, as I taught a group about spiritual gifts and introduced the folk to the Gift Giver, a woman finds her relationship with God transformed because she didn't realise, she could have relationship (or fellowship, as Paul calls it) with the Holy Spirit.

'You mean you can just speak to Him?' she asked, incredulous. 'Why has no one ever told me this?'

The Holy Spirit is not the weaker Partner in the God-Head; He really is God. Historically, men and women who encountered the uniqueness of God through the Spirit have been labelled 'mystic.' We often label what we don't understand, and by labelling Christian men and women of God who lost the ability to compartmentalise through encountering the Presence of God 'mystic', we can create a barrier of misunderstanding and wariness.

If you're curious to learn more about walking in the Spirit, read books by Christian mystics like Madam Guyon, Julian of Norwich, Brother Lawrence, etc. Not because you want to explore mysticism, but because it's valuable to explore stories of men and women who practiced the pursuit of God and discovered the reality and power of life with the Holy Spirit.

'We have so much to learn, and so much more to unlearn.' *Word of Wisdom*

You may have heard of Nicholas Herman of Lorraine (circa 1614-1691), or Brother Lawrence, as he is more commonly known. Nicholas was a lay brother at a Paris monastery. He was converted at the age of 18 when he saw a tree stripped of its leaves in the winter and thought of how it would soon be renewed and come back to life. An uneducated man who had been a soldier and a footman, he worked in the monastery kitchens washing pots, cooking and cleaning. Practising the Presence of God led him to become full of wisdom and find joy in the mundane and laborious. He lived for God, and not just with God. He taught himself to abide until abiding in God became like breathing to him. His book, *The Practice of the Presence of God*, is well worth a read.

Can we bring God into all we do and live in a God-conscious, rather than self-centred way? Can we surrender everything to Him and for Him?

7. Be Filled

> *'Be very careful, then, how you live—not as unwise but as wise, making the most of every opportunity, because the days are evil. Therefore, do not be foolish, but understand what the Lord's will is. Do not get drunk on wine, which leads to debauchery.* ***Instead, be filled with the Spirit****...' Ephesians 5:15-18*

Various scholars point out that the Greek imperative tense is used for 'be filled' in this verse, which implies that being filled is not a one-off event, but an ongoing state. We go on being filled. Jesus tells us to ask the Father for more of the Holy Spirit, promising that we won't be disappointed (Luke 11:13).

If we want to experience, feel, touch, know, sense, and live inside God's love, we have to be filled with the Spirit. If you want to see yourself, your family, church, neighbourhood, nation, and this planet changed, be filled with the Spirit.

> *'And hope does not put us to shame, because God's love has been poured out into our hearts through the Holy Spirit, who has been given to us.' Romans 5:5*

We experience love through the Spirit. Ask Father to fill you with the Spirit. You aren't excluded. Ask the Holy Spirit to fill you with more each day. He gives, without discriminating, the infilling Jesus earned for you.

Look at this explosive verse:

> *'"For the one whom God has sent speaks the words of God, for God gives the Spirit without limit."' John 3:34*

The Spirit without limit!

AND FINALLY

Just as I was told by the prophet in Africa, I am telling you now:

The Holy Spirit longs to have a relationship with you.

Talk with and listen to the Spirit of the Father, the Spirit of Jesus: The Holy Spirit.

Give Love A-Way

APPENDICES INDEX

APPENDIX 1: Ministry School Student Listens to Father God

The homework for a group of Ministry School students was to sit with a sheet of blank paper and a pen, and to simply ask the Father what He wanted to say. The student heard and wrote about a banqueting table. It was the first time she had encountered God in this way.

APPENDIX 2: Moses and Five Limiting Beliefs

Chart detailing Moses Five Limiting Beliefs from Chapter 8. Which of these limiting beliefs might hinder you?

APPENDIX 1:

Ministry School Student Listens to Father God

I saw a huge banqueting table filled with food, drink, colourful flowers and fruit.

God said:

"I have prepared this for you: all you have to do is eat and drink and enjoy the flavours and the sustenance. It is all done for you. Just enjoy. No need to strive and prepare. It's done. So, eat, feast and experience the taste, sight and textures.

Then come – sit with Me and relax. Let's talk like old friends after a shared meal. Let's sit comfortably together. Let the food slowly digest. Let it become part of you. Let it build, transform and heal you from within.

Let it feed your body.
Let it feed your mind.
Let it feed your spirit.

In physical terms, you do not understand how the food you eat sustains your body or affects your mind. So it is with My spiritual food. You don't have to understand it, just eat and enjoy and let it minister to you. Let it transform you. Let it bless you.

..... Don't struggle to understand it - enjoy. Be at peace with what I am doing. Full and beautiful Shalom Peace."

APPENDIX 2:

Moses and Five Limiting Beliefs

BROKEN IDENTITY	THE DISEASE	THE FEAR	THE SOLUTION
But who am I? Exodus 3:11	Low Self Esteem	God Can't Use Me	'I WILL BE WITH YOU.' Exodus 3:12 Matthew 28:20
I don't know You well enough (I'm not ready) Exodus 3:13	Anxiety	God Isn't Powerful	'I AM WHO I AM.' Exodus 3:14 John 14:6
But what if? Exodus 4:1	Worry	God Isn't Big Enough	'... THESE SIGNS SHALL ACCOMPANY YOU.' Exodus 4:8 Mark 16:17
I am not equipped Exodus 4:10	Limiting self-beliefs	God Isn't Enough for Me	HELP AND TEACHING (The Holy Spirit) Exodus 4:13 John 14:16 & 26
Others are better than me Exodus 4:13	Pride	God Isn't Truthful	YOU AREN'T ALONE Exodus 3:11 Matthew 6:33

Give Love A-Way

Printed in Great Britain
by Amazon